HOW TO SECURE GOVERNMENT CONTRACTS

How To Secure Government Contracts
Jerrell Johnson Jr.

ISBN 979-8-89691-923-0

HOW TO SECURE GOVERNMENT CONTRACTS

SELLING TO THE GOVERNMENT: A COMPREHENSIVE GUIDE

JERRELL JOHNSON JR.

THANK YOU.

Dear Friends, Mentors, Competitors, Contracting Specialists, and Contracting Officers,

As I take a moment to reflect on my journey in the intricate world of government contracting, I am overwhelmed with gratitude for each and every one of you who has crossed my path. From my earliest days in this challenging field, your guidance, rivalry, expertise, and oversight have profoundly shaped my career and personal growth.

To my mentors, thank you for sharing your wisdom and insights so generously. Your encouragement and advice have been the guiding lights during my most challenging moments. You taught me not just the nuances of contracting but also the values of integrity, perseverance, and community that are essential to our field.

To my competitors, thank you for pushing me to exceed my limits and strive for excellence. Each competition we engaged in was a learning opportunity, helping me to sharpen my skills and rethink my strategies. You have been invaluable in driving me to be innovative and resilient, qualities that have been crucial in navigating the complexities of our industry.

To the many contracting specialists, your expertise and dedication to the intricacies of contract law and administration have been nothing short of inspiring. Thank you for your patience and diligence, which ensure that every contract we undertake is executed with precision and fairness.

And to the contracting officers, thank you for your fairness and steadfast adherence to the principles that govern our work. Your commitment to transparency and accountability has not only fostered a trustful working environment but has also instilled in me a profound respect for the responsibilities we share in serving our community and country.

Each of you has left an indelible mark on my life and career. The lessons learned and friendships forged during our collaborations will be cherished forever. As I continue on this path, I carry with me not just the knowledge and experiences gained but also a deep sense of gratitude and respect for all of you.

Thank you for being a part of my journey. I look forward to many more years of learning from and working with you, as we strive together to achieve excellence in all that we do.

With deepest appreciation and respect,

Jerrell Johnson Jr.

CONTENTS

FOREWORD

Winning a government contract is just the beginning; knowing how to navigate the aftermath is crucial. This guide offers essential tips to help you kick off a government contract, manage performance evaluations, handle changes and claims, and secure proper payment. It details strategies for ensuring your performance is accurately reported and provides insights applicable to both Federal contracts and the wider government marketplace. Whether you're a seasoned contractor looking to polish your administrative skills or new to the field and eager to grasp the basics, this booklet is designed to inform and inspire you to master the nuances of government contracting.

These tips are designed to help contractors understand how a government contract is kicked off, how your performance will be judged, how contract changes and claims are to be handled, and how to respond to remedies. That might be applied to how to invoice and get paid and how to ensure that your performance is properly reported. Note that while some tips are specifically for Federal contracts, all of the principles described in this book apply within the broader government Marketplace.

Please remember that this booklet contains only basic facts. If you are an experienced government contractor, the booklet should reinforce good contract Administration practices. If you are less experienced, it will alert you to the fundamentals and perhaps inspire you to learn more.

Figure 1 Jerrell Johnson Jr. and Kevin Harrington of "Shark Tank" discuss the merits of Nijsha Enterprise Inc.

PREFACE

By Jerrell Johnson Jr.

Government contracting is one of the most powerful yet misunderstood opportunities for entrepreneurs. When I first ventured into this space, I quickly realized that knowledge—not just ambition—is the key to success. The complexities of federal procurement, the intricate regulations, and the competitive nature of securing contracts can be overwhelming. However, I also discovered that with the right strategy, guidance, and persistence, small businesses can not only survive but thrive in the federal marketplace.

MEETINGS ARE KEY

Jerrell Johnson meets with the legal advocates at New Orleans 8a Conference in New Orleans,LA 2020.

Throughout my career, I've encountered countless business owners, industry professionals, and contracting officers who were willing to

share their expertise, lessons learned, and strategies for success. I realized that, like me, many entrepreneurs were navigating this industry with limited resources, little guidance, and a desire to learn from those who had done it before. I wanted to create a resource that simplifies the process, demystifies the language, and empowers business owners to confidently compete for and win government contracts.

The writing process for this book has been a collaborative effort, combining real-world experience with insights from top industry professionals. I've had the privilege of working alongside seasoned contracting specialists, procurement officers, and successful government contractors who contributed key pointers, strategies, and cautionary lessons that every entrepreneur should know. Their input has been invaluable in ensuring that this book is not just theoretical—but a practical, actionable guide for any business owner looking to break into or scale within the government contracting space.

This book is for the aspiring entrepreneur who has heard of government contracts but doesn't know where to start. It is for the small business owner who has bid on contracts but struggles to win them. It is for the established company looking to refine its strategy and build long-term success in federal procurementSuccess in government contracting is not about luck. It's about knowledge, preparation, and persistence. If you are willing to invest the time to learn, adapt, and strategically position yourself, there is no limit to what you can achieve in this space. I hope this book serves as a roadmap that guides you toward sustainable growth, competitive success, and lasting impact in the world of government contracting.

Let's get to work.

Jerrell Johnson Jr.

INTRODUCTION

A Roadmap to Securing Government Contracts

Jerrell Johnson at his office.

The world of government contracting is vast, competitive, and full of opportunity. Every year, the U.S. government awards billions of dollars in contracts to businesses of all sizes, providing them with stable revenue streams, opportunities for growth, and an unparalleled level of credibility in their industries. However, the journey to winning a government contract is not as simple as submitting a bid—it requires strategy, preparation, and a deep understanding of the contracting process.

This book is designed to be your **roadmap** for navigating the government contracting space, from understanding the fundamentals to developing winning strategies. Whether you are a small business owner looking to enter the government marketplace for the first time or an experienced contractor seeking to refine your approach, this guide provides actionable insights, step-by-step strategies, and real-world examples to help you succeed.

What This Book Covers

Government contracting can be overwhelming for newcomers, and even experienced professionals often struggle to keep up with evolving policies, regulations, and competitive dynamics. That's why this book is structured to guide you through every stage of the process, from identifying opportunities to executing contracts successfully.

Here's what you'll learn:

- **The Basics of Government Contracting** – Understand the different types of contracts, how the federal procurement process works, and how to position your business for success.
- **Operating in Multiple NAICS Codes** – Learn how businesses can strategically bid in different sectors while maintaining their small business status.
- **Capture Management Strategies** – Discover how to proactively identify, assess, and position yourself for contract opportunities before they are even solicited.
- **Proposal Development & Pricing to Win** – Master the art of writing compelling proposals that meet government requirements while remaining competitive.
- **The Shipley Associates Color Team Process** – Learn how top government contractors refine and optimize their proposals using a structured review system.
- **Post-Bid and Contract Execution** – Gain insights into

handling government contract performance, evaluations, modifications, and compliance.

- **Lessons for Small Businesses** – Get practical guidance on leveraging resources, strategic outsourcing, and business development tactics to scale your government contracting operations.

How to Use This Book

This book is not meant to be read once and set aside. Instead, think of it as a **playbook**—a reference guide that you can return to at different stages of your government contracting journey. Whether you are preparing for your first bid or refining your pricing strategy for a major contract, you'll find strategies, tips, and frameworks to help you navigate the complexities of the process.

Each chapter is structured to **build on the previous one**, ensuring that readers at all levels can follow a logical progression from foundational knowledge to advanced strategies. **Case studies, real-world examples, and expert insights** are included throughout to illustrate key concepts and provide practical applications.

The Path Forward

Government contracting is not a field for those looking for quick wins—it requires patience, persistence, and a strategic approach. **Success is not about luck; it is about preparation.** The companies that consistently win contracts are the ones that have mastered the process, developed strong relationships, and built a reputation for delivering quality solutions.

The strategies and frameworks outlined in this book will **equip you with the knowledge and tools to position your business for long-term success** in the government marketplace. If you are willing to put in the work, refine your approach, and continually improve, the opportunities are limitless.

Let's begin the journey toward **securing your first—or next—government contract**.

CHAPTER 1
THE PURSUIT OF GOVERNMENT CONTRACTS

PURSUIT REQUIRES ENGAGEMENT

Nijsha Enterprise display at New Orleans 8a Conference in New Orleans, LA 2020.

Pursuing government contracts, as underscored by the aphorism attributed to Willie Sutton regarding his bank robberies—"because that's where the money is"—epitomizes the pragmatic allure of the government marketplace for businesses. Indeed, the U.S. government is a colossal entity with a procurement budget that extends into the hundreds of billions annually, representing a substantial market opportunity for companies of all sizes.

The motivation for companies like Perdue to engage in government contracting extends beyond the sheer volume of financial opportunities available. Government contracts offer a reliable revenue stream that can be more stable compared to the private sector, especially during periods of economic downturn. This stability derives from the government's ongoing need for diverse goods and services, irrespective of broader economic conditions, ensuring a consistent demand that companies like Perdue can capitalize on.

Moreover, government contracts can also serve as a platform for business growth and expansion. For small and medium-sized enterprises, or even larger corporations, these contracts can help in scaling operations, improving technical capabilities, and enhancing market credibility. Successfully executing a government contract can also serve as a testament to a company's reliability and quality, enhancing its credentials and making it more competitive both in and beyond the government sector.

Additionally, engaging with the government can provide businesses with access to new networks and partnerships. The complex and varied requirements of government contracts often necessitate collaboration with a range of stakeholders, including other businesses, which can lead to synergistic partnerships that extend beyond individual contracts.

Government contracting also encourages companies to adhere to higher standards of compliance and operational excellence. The rigorous requirements for transparency, reporting, and performance in government contracts can help businesses streamline their processes and adopt best practices that improve overall efficiency and effectiveness.

However, the pursuit of government contracts is not without its challenges. The process can be intricate, requiring a deep understanding of specific procurement rules and regulations. Companies must navigate a competitive bidding process, adhere to strict compliance standards, and often manage more complex administrative processes than those in the private sector.

While the pursuit of government contracts presents significant opportunities for revenue and growth, it also requires a strategic approach that encompasses thorough preparation, robust compliance frameworks, and an understanding of the nuances of government procurement. For companies like Perdue, these contracts represent not just a substantial revenue opportunity but also a chance to enhance their operational capabilities and strategic positioning in a broad marketplace.

APPLYING THIS KNOWLEDGE TO SMALL BUSINESSES

Applying the knowledge in this book, to your business, will require many hours of study, preparation, marketing, writing, and pricing exercises. Since many of the readers of this book will likely be small businesses, I wanted to ensure you understood how the government classifies small businesses.

In the context of U.S. government contracting, the definition of a "small business" is a crucial aspect for firms aspiring to take advantage of specific provisions and opportunities tailored to them. According to the Small Business Administration (SBA), a small business is defined not only by its earnings or number of employees but also by its independence, operational characteristics, and the industry in which it competes.

The SBA establishes size standards that vary across industries to reflect the economic differences among various sectors. These standards are expressed either in terms of average annual receipts or the number of employees. A business must meet these size requirements to qualify for federal government programs designed for small businesses, including contracting opportunities meant to foster small business growth and competitiveness in the wider economy.

To determine if a business qualifies as small, it can reference the North American Industry Classification System (NAICS) codes, which are matched to size standards on the SBA's website. Each industry classified under NAICS has a corresponding size standard that, when exceeded, disqualifies a company from being considered small. For instance, architectural firms may be classified as small if their annual receipts are under $4.5 million, whereas a manufacturer of guided missiles and space vehicles might be considered small if it has fewer than 1,000 employees.

Small businesses are often seen as a cornerstone of the American economy, and their classification allows them to benefit from various government-led initiatives. These initiatives include targeted access to contracts through set-asides, where certain contracts are exclusively reserved for competitive bidding among small businesses to enhance their chances of winning federal business without facing competition from larger, possibly multinational corporations.

The SBA's size standards are designed to reflect economic and industry variations, ensuring a level playing field that acknowledges the unique challenges small businesses face. It's essential for small business owners and managers to accurately understand and frequently review these standards as they can and do change, impacting eligibility for federal programs.

For more detailed guidance and the latest updates on small business standards, one should regularly consult the SBA's website or directly access the page detailing size standards at SBA Size Standards. This resource is critical for ensuring that a business remains informed about its classification and the opportunities that classification may afford under federal contracting regulations.

Companies can operate under multiple North American Industry Classification System (NAICS) codes and still retain their status as small businesses in the eyes of the government, depending on the diversity of their services or products and the specific size standards associated with each NAICS code.

Operating in Multiple NAICS Codes

1. **Diverse Business Operations**: Companies often engage in varied business activities that span different sectors or industries. For instance, a company might provide IT services (classified under one NAICS code) while also manufacturing computer hardware (classified under another NAICS code). Each of these activities corresponds to a different NAICS code with its own specific size standards.
2. **Size Standards Variation**: The SBA sets distinct size standards for different industries based on factors like market conditions and industry characteristics. These standards are typically expressed in terms of the number of employees or annual receipts. A company could be considered small in one industry but not in another if it operates under multiple NAICS codes.

Strategic Advantages

Operating under multiple NAICS codes offers several strategic advantages:

1. **Broader Market Opportunities**: By qualifying as a small business under multiple NAICS codes, companies can access a wider range of government set-asides or contracting opportunities specifically reserved for small businesses in various industries.
2. **Flexibility in Bidding**: Companies can bid on different types of government contracts that require specific industry classifications, thereby maximizing their chances of winning contracts and expanding their business operations.

3. **Risk Diversification**: Engaging in business activities across various sectors helps diversify income sources and reduce dependency on a single market, which can buffer the company against industry-specific downturns.

Compliance and Verification

While there are advantages, companies must carefully manage their operations to ensure compliance:

1. **Accurate NAICS Code Assignment**: Companies must ensure that they are operating under the correct NAICS codes that accurately reflect their primary business activities. This often requires analyzing which aspects of their operations generate the most revenue or where the majority of their employees are engaged.
2. **Regular Review of Size Standards**: The SBA periodically reviews and adjusts size standards. Companies must regularly check these standards to ensure they still qualify as small businesses under their respective NAICS codes.
3. **Verification During Contracting**: When bidding for government contracts, companies must certify their size status based on the specific NAICS code applicable to the solicitation. Misrepresentation can lead to penalties, including contract termination and legal consequences.

Operating under multiple NAICS codes allows companies to maintain flexibility in their business operations and take full advantage of government contracting opportunities designated for small businesses. However, it requires diligent management and constant review of SBA size standards to ensure ongoing compliance and optimal strategic positioning in the government marketplace.

Once you have identified your NAICS and designed your company's business model, you have to begin the process of capturing business. Capture management, pricing to win, as well as proposal management and proposal writing, will become your chief concerns to secure government contracts.

Developing a systematic and meticulous business methodology forms the cornerstone of success in securing government contracts. The journey to winning such contracts is heavily anchored in mastering a blend of strategic disciplines including capture management, competitive pricing strategies, robust proposal management, and skilled proposal writing. Each of these components plays a crucial role and must be integrated effectively to enhance a company's chances of securing government contracts.

Capture Management serves as the strategic foundation for the entire contracting process. This approach is about identifying potential opportunities early, understanding customer requirements, and tailoring your company's offerings to meet those needs. It involves a thorough analysis of the competitive landscape and developing relationships with key stakeholders to enhance the potential for success. This proactive engagement helps in shaping procurement opportunities before they are formally solicited, which is critical in positioning a company favorably against competitors.

Pricing to Win is another essential strategy. It requires not only understanding the cost baseline from an internal perspective but also the market conditions and pricing strategies of competitors. It's about setting a price that is competitive, but also ensures profitability. This strategic pricing involves a nuanced understanding of both the cost structure of one's services and the pricing tolerance of the government agency involved.

Proposal Management and **Proposal Writing** are the stages where strategic preparation transitions into actionable bids. Effective proposal management ensures that the bidding process is aligned with the company's strategic goals and that all proposals meet the stringent compliance requirements of government RFPs. It involves coordinating various teams to produce a coherent document that addresses all technical, managerial, and logistical aspects of the RFP.

Proposal writing, meanwhile, is the craft of articulating a company's offer in a way that is not only compliant with the solicitation requirements but compelling enough to stand out. This skill is about more than just meeting the basic criteria; it's about presenting a convincing narrative that demonstrates a deep understanding of the customer's needs and outlines clear, measurable benefits that resonate with the decision-makers.

By systematically applying these methodologies—capturing the right information, pricing strategically, managing proposals effectively, and writing compelling bids—companies can significantly increase their likelihood of not just competing, but winning government contracts. This structured approach ensures that every step from the initial market analysis to the final proposal submission is executed with precision, aligning closely with the governmental agency's objectives and thus positioning the company as the best choice for the contract.

Success in government contracting is highly dependent on continuous improvement and learning from each proposal cycle. Companies must not only execute well on current proposals but also gather intelligence and refine their strategies for future opportunities. This requires a robust system for capturing lessons learned and integrating this knowledge back into the business strategy and operational tactics.

Continuous Learning and Adaptation are crucial. Each contract bid, whether won or lost, provides valuable insights. Effective companies analyze what worked, what didn't, and how they can improve their process for identifying and capturing opportunities. This might involve adjusting capture strategies, refining pricing models, or improving proposal content and presentation.

Technological Integration also plays a significant role. In the digital age, leveraging technology to enhance the accuracy and efficiency of proposal development is essential. Tools that facilitate better collaboration among dispersed teams, manage documents more efficiently, and allow for the real-time tracking of proposal status are invaluable. Furthermore, advanced analytics can provide deeper insights into market trends, competitor analysis, and customer preferences.

Stakeholder Engagement remains a continuous theme throughout the capture management life-cycle. Maintaining strong relationships with all stakeholders—especially within government agencies—helps in gaining critical insights that can influence proposal strategies. Engaging stakeholders through regular communication, feedback loops, and participation in industry events can help firms stay aligned with current needs and anticipate future requirements.

In sum, developing a robust business methodology that emphasizes systematic capture management, competitive pricing, effective proposal management, and skilled proposal writing is indispensable. These disciplines are interconnected, each feeding into and bolstering the others, creating a comprehensive approach that significantly increases the likelihood of securing government contracts. This strategic integration, backed by continuous learning and technological support, ensures that companies not only survive but thrive in the competitive government contracting arena.

CHAPTER 2

INTEGRATING THE SHIPLEY ASSOCIATES COLOR TEAM PROCESS

Figure 2 Source: https:amplioservoces.com/intropricetowintraining

A successful government contracting strategy requires a structured approach that aligns Capture Management, Proposal Development, and Post-Bid Activities. By integrating the **Shipley Associates Color Team Process**, businesses can improve their win probability by ensuring that all stages—from identifying opportunities to contract fulfillment—are executed with precision and alignment to customer needs.

CAPTURE MANAGEMENT AND PRE-PROPOSAL STRATEGY

The first step in the contracting lifecycle is Capture Management, where companies identify, assess, and position themselves for upcoming opportunities. During this phase, the **White Team** plays a crucial role in setting the overall strategy. This team consists of senior executives and key stakeholders who analyze market trends, agency budgets, procurement forecasts, and competitor positioning. The White Team ensures that the opportunity aligns with the company's long-term goals before significant resources are committed.

THE SHIPLEY ASSOCIATES AND NIJSHA ENTERPRISE'S WHITE TEAM PROCESS: SETTING THE STRATEGIC FOUNDATION FOR GOVERNMENT CONTRACTING

The Shipley Associates White Team Process plays a foundational role in Capture Management, the first and most critical phase in the government contracting lifecycle. This stage determines whether a company will pursue an opportunity by aligning it with organizational capabilities, market positioning, and long-term strategic objectives. Before a single proposal is drafted, before resources are committed, and before the company decides to move forward, the White Team assesses whether the opportunity is worth the investment.

The Role of the White Team in Capture Management

Unlike the other Shipley Color Teams, which focus on refining and reviewing the proposal itself, the White Team operates at the executive level, where big-picture thinking and long-term strategy drive decision-making. Comprised of senior executives, key stakeholders, and capture managers, this team is responsible for identifying opportunities that align with the company's capabilities, market strengths, and financial growth plan.

Figure 3 Deciding who does what in Capture and Proposal Mangement

The White Team's primary function is to conduct a high-level strategic review before engaging in a full capture effort. They ensure that the opportunity:

- Aligns with the company's mission, expertise, and growth strategy
- Has a high probability of win (Pwin) based on market conditions and competitor analysis
- Fits within the company's budgetary constraints and resource availability
- Positions the company effectively for future opportunities and contract expansions

Key Responsibilities of the White Team

1. **Market Intelligence and Competitive Landscape Analysis**

The White Team conducts extensive research into the agency's procurement history, budget allocation, and upcoming spending priorities. This includes evaluating:

- Government procurement forecasts and spending trends
- Previous contract awards and incumbents in the space
- Competitor positioning and their past performance on similar contracts
- Political and economic factors that could impact funding or procurement priorities

Understanding these factors helps the team determine whether the government agency has a strong and continued need for the services being offered and whether the company has a realistic chance of securing the contract.

2. **Opportunity Qualification and Strategic Fit**

Once potential contract opportunities are identified, the White Team must determine whether pursuing them aligns with the company's strategic objectives. This involves asking:

- Does this contract align with our core competencies and business goals?
- Does it position us for future opportunities in this agency or sector?
- Can we commit the necessary resources without overextending our company?

- How will this opportunity affect our long-term financial and operational health?

The answers to these questions dictate whether the company will proceed with the opportunity or redirect its resources elsewhere.

3. **Evaluating the Probability of Win (Pwin) and Risk Assessment**

One of the most crucial functions of the White Team is determining the Probability of Win (Pwin)—the likelihood of securing the contract. The team analyzes:

- Past performance data on similar contracts
- Strength of existing agency relationships
- Competitive differentiation (what makes the company's offering unique)
- Potential risks such as cost overruns, compliance issues, and changing government regulations

If the White Team determines that the Pwin is high enough to justify the investment, the company moves forward into Capture Planning. If the risks outweigh the potential benefits, resources are redirected to more viable opportunities.

4. **Defining the Capture Strategy**

If the opportunity passes the strategic fit and risk assessment stage, the White Team begins shaping the company's Capture Plan. This includes:

- Positioning the company as the preferred contractor by engaging with agency decision-makers

- Identifying potential teaming partners or subcontractors to strengthen the proposal
- Developing key win themes that will be central to the proposal's messaging
- Building a preliminary pricing strategy to ensure competitiveness

At this stage, the White Team ensures that all subsequent proposal efforts are grounded in a well-defined strategy, giving the company a clear competitive advantage before the formal solicitation is even released.

The White Team's Role in the Decision-Making Process

Ultimately, the White Team holds the authority to approve or reject an opportunity. Their strategic insight prevents wasted resources, unrealistic pursuits, and missed opportunities. If an opportunity is greenlit, the White Team hands off their strategic findings to the Capture Manager, who then executes the Capture Plan and works with the Proposal Teams (Pink, Red, and Gold Teams) to refine and submit a winning proposal.

Why the White Team Process Matters

Without the rigorous strategic assessment conducted by the White Team, companies risk chasing contracts that do not align with their strengths, investing in proposals with a low chance of success, and failing to differentiate themselves in a crowded market. By implementing a disciplined White Team process, businesses can:

- Ensure smarter bid/no-bid decisions
- Maximize their win probability (Pwin)
- Improve resource allocation and financial planning
- Strengthen long-term positioning in the federal marketplace

Final Thoughts

The Shipley Associates White Team Process is a critical first step in government contracting success. It ensures that companies only pursue high-value, strategically aligned opportunities that offer real potential for growth. By leveraging market intelligence, evaluating risk, and refining capture strategies early, the White Team sets the foundation for profitable, long-term contracting success.

For companies looking to scale in the federal space, mastering Capture Management and the White Team Process is not just beneficial—it's essential.

THE SHIPLEY ASSOCIATES BLUE TEAM PROCESS: DEFINING THE CAPTURE STRATEGY AND INFLUENCING THE RFP

Figure 4 Capture Planning requires strong communication

Once an opportunity is identified and approved by the White Team, the focus shifts to Capture Management, where the Blue Team plays a pivotal role. This phase is all about positioning the company for success before the government releases the Request for Proposal (RFP). A well-executed Blue Team process can significantly enhance the company's Probability of Win (Pwin) by shaping the opportunity, gathering intelligence, and developing a customer-focused capture strategy.

The Purpose of the Blue Team

The Blue Team ensures that the company is fully prepared before the RFP is released by focusing on three main objectives:

1. Developing a strong capture strategy that differentiates the company from competitors.
2. Gathering customer intelligence to align solutions with the agency's specific needs.
3. Refining customer engagement efforts to proactively influence the RFP's structure and requirements.

By acting early, before the formal solicitation is published, the Blue Team positions the company as a preferred contractor and maximizes its ability to submit a competitive, customer-focused proposal.

Key Responsibilities of the Blue Team

1. **Defining the Capture Strategy**

The Blue Team works closely with the Capture Manager to outline a detailed strategy that dictates how the company will compete for and win the contract. This includes:

- Identifying key decision-makers and stakeholders within the government agency.

- Understanding procurement objectives, pain points, and agency priorities.
- Determining competitive advantages by assessing internal strengths and weaknesses.
- Developing preliminary win themes that address customer needs and align with evaluation criteria.

The **Capture Strategy Document**, developed by the Blue Team, serves as the foundation for all subsequent proposal efforts.

2. Gathering and Analyzing Customer Intelligence

A winning bid is customer-driven, not company-driven. The Blue Team conducts in-depth customer research to ensure that the proposal speaks directly to the needs and priorities of the agency. This includes:

- Conducting meetings and outreach with agency decision-makers to gather insights on expectations.
- Reviewing past RFPs, contracts, and procurement trends to understand historical buying behavior.
- Leveraging industry networks and advisory boards for insider knowledge on upcoming solicitations.
- Building relationships with government representatives to ensure alignment between their goals and the company's solution.

This intelligence gathering allows the company to pre-position itself as the ideal contractor before the competition even begins.

3. Competitive Analysis and Market Positioning

To increase its Probability of Win (Pwin), the Blue Team must understand the competition. This involves:

- Identifying competitors likely to bid and analyzing their strengths and weaknesses.
- Conducting Black Hat Reviews, where the team role-plays as competitors to anticipate their strategies.
- Assessing pricing trends and technical capabilities of competing firms.
- Determining gaps in the market that the company can leverage to its advantage.

Through this analysis, the Blue Team refines the company's approach and strengthens its differentiation strategy.

4. **Influencing the RFP Before Release**

One of the most strategic roles of the Blue Team is to shape the government's solicitation in favor of the company's strengths. By engaging with decision-makers early, the team can:

- Suggest key performance metrics and evaluation criteria that highlight the company's capabilities.
- Clarify technical requirements that align with the company's strengths.
- Encourage the inclusion of specific contract vehicles or past performance criteria that the company meets.

If done effectively, this influence ensures that the RFP plays to the company's strengths, giving it a significant competitive edge.

5. **Refining the Pwin Assessment and Solution Framework**

The Probability of Win (Pwin) assessment is a dynamic calculation that evolves throughout Capture Management. The Blue Team refines this assessment by:

- Analyzing new intelligence gathered from customer engagements.
- Revising risk assessments and pricing strategies based on market trends.
- Ensuring that the technical and management approach aligns with agency priorities.

Additionally, the solution framework is defined, outlining the technical approach, staffing strategy, pricing model, and compliance requirements.

The Blue Team's Role in the Capture Decision

The work of the Blue Team culminates in a formal Capture Review, where executive leadership decides whether to fully pursue the opportunity or shift resources to a higher-priority contract. If the Capture Plan is strong and leadership approves the pursuit, the opportunity transitions to the Proposal Phase, where the Pink, Red, and Gold Teams refine the actual submission.

Why the Blue Team Process Matters

A strong Blue Team process increases the likelihood of success by pre-positioning the company as the government's best choice. Without this step, companies risk entering the proposal phase unprepared, reacting to the RFP instead of shaping it. By focusing on early engagement, intelligence gathering, and competitive positioning, the Blue Team lays the groundwork for a winning proposal.

For companies looking to consistently win federal contracts, mastering the Blue Team process is not optional—it's essential.

THE SHIPLEY ASSOCIATES PINK TEAM PROCESS: STRUCTURING THE PROPOSAL FOR COMPLIANCE AND COMPETITIVE STRENGTH

Proposal Development and Refinement

Jerrell Johnson at Porshe, securing a contract for Nijsha Enterprise to produce vehicle cables.

As soon as the RFP is released, proposal development begins with the Pink Team, which performs the first comprehensive review of the draft proposal outline. The Pink Team ensures that the solution framework aligns with the government's stated requirements, customer hot buttons, and evaluation criteria. Their review focuses on compliance, clarity, and structure to prevent misalignment between the technical and management approaches.

The Pink Team Process is a foundational step in Shipley Associates' proposal development lifecycle, serving as the first comprehensive review after an RFP (Request for Proposal) is released. While the Blue Team works on shaping the pre-RFP capture strategy and the Black Team evaluates competitors, the Pink Team ensures that the initial proposal draft is structured properly, aligns with the agency's requirements, and is strategically positioned to win. This process is essential for setting the direction of the proposal before significant writing and development occur. A well-executed Pink Team review minimizes costly last-minute changes and ensures that the document is built on a strong framework from the outset.

The Pink Team is responsible for validating the overall structure and compliance of the proposal. The first step in this process is a detailed review of the RFP to ensure that the proposal's structure fully aligns with the government's stated requirements, evaluation criteria, and key performance indicators. Government agencies have strict formatting and organizational guidelines that must be met, and failure to adhere to these specifications can result in disqualification. The Pink Team cross-references the draft proposal with the RFP to verify that every section, attachment, and supporting document is accounted for. This includes verifying page limits, required certifications, past performance narratives, and compliance with federal regulations such as FAR (Federal Acquisition Regulation) and DFARS (Defense Federal Acquisition Regulation Supplement).

A key focus of the Pink Team review is customer alignment. Winning proposals are not just about demonstrating technical expertise; they must also reflect a deep understanding of the customer's mission, priorities, and concerns. The Pink Team assesses whether the draft proposal adequately addresses customer hot buttons, pain points, and strategic objectives. This involves evaluating whether the executive summary, win themes, and solution framework effectively convey the company's ability to meet the government's needs. If gaps exist between what the customer is looking for and what the draft proposal presents, the Pink Team provides recommendations to refine the messaging and strengthen alignment.

Another critical role of the Pink Team is evaluating the proposal's organization and logical flow. Government evaluators read multiple proposals in a short timeframe, meaning that clarity and readability are just as important as technical accuracy. The Pink Team ensures that the narrative is easy to follow, key messages are highlighted, and supporting evidence is structured logically. They assess whether the technical and management approaches are effectively integrated, preventing a situation where the technical solution is strong but lacks a coherent management plan, or vice versa. The team looks for redundancies, missing information, and inconsistencies that could weaken the overall submission.

The solution framework is another major area of focus for the Pink Team. In federal contracting, proposals must present a clear, detailed plan for how the contractor will meet the government's requirements. The Pink Team evaluates whether the solution is well-defined, technically sound, and achievable within the constraints of the contract. This includes assessing whether staffing levels are appropriate, subcontractor roles are clearly defined, risk mitigation strategies are in place, and compliance requirements are addressed. The team also checks that the pricing strategy—although not finalized until later stages—is realistic and aligns with the technical solution and performance expectations.

In addition to compliance and structure, the Pink Team evaluates the draft proposal for competitiveness. A proposal that is compliant but fails to differentiate the company from competitors is unlikely to win. The team ensures that the draft proposal highlights the company's unique strengths, past performance, and innovative approaches. This includes verifying that the executive summary is compelling and customer-focused, win themes are emphasized throughout the document, and past performance narratives effectively demonstrate relevant experience. If weaknesses are identified, the Pink Team provides actionable feedback to enhance the proposal's competitiveness and persuasive impact.

The Pink Team review is conducted as a structured, iterative process. The team provides detailed feedback on each section of the proposal, offering specific guidance on compliance, clarity, alignment with customer needs, and competitive positioning. Proposal writers then revise the draft based on this feedback, ensuring that the next version is stronger and more refined. This cycle continues until the proposal reaches a level of quality where it can advance to Red Team review, which focuses on finalizing content for submission.

A strong Pink Team process reduces the risk of major rewrites later in the proposal development cycle. By ensuring that the initial draft is strategically sound, technically compliant, and aligned with customer needs, the Pink Team sets the stage for a winning proposal. Organizations that invest time and effort into a thorough Pink Team review ultimately produce higher-quality proposals with a greater likelihood of success in government contracting.

THE SHIPLEY ASSOCIATES RED TEAM PROCESS: ENSURING A WINNING, COMPLIANT, AND PERSUASIVE PROPOSAL

The Red Team Process is one of the most critical components of Shipley Associates' proposal development methodology. It is the final and most rigorous review stage before a proposal is submitted, ensuring that every aspect of the document is compliant, compelling, and optimized for success. While earlier color teams, such as the Pink Team, focus on structure, clarity, and ensuring alignment with the government's requirements, the Red Team's purpose is to evaluate the proposal from the perspective of the customer and the evaluators. This ensures that the submission is not just a compliant document, but a winning proposal that differentiates the company from the competition.

SEIZE THE MOMENT!

Jerrell Johnson presenting Nijsha Enterprise, Inc.'s products at a trade show.

Once the Pink Team has completed the initial review and provided recommendations, the Proposal Team refines the draft, addressing identified gaps, improving win themes, and strengthening compliance with the RFP (Request for Proposal) criteria. At this stage, the Red Team is brought in to perform a high-level, independent review of the near-final proposal. The Red Team consists of senior executives, subject matter experts (SMEs), former contracting officers, and individuals who were not involved in drafting the document. The purpose of using an independent review team is to simulate the mindset of the government's proposal evaluators, ensuring that the submission is clear, persuasive, and structured to receive the highest possible score.

The first key objective of the Red Team is to evaluate the proposal for compliance with the government's requirements. Federal proposals must adhere to strict guidelines regarding content, formatting, technical accuracy, and contractual language, as specified in the RFP. Any non-compliance can lead to disqualification, making this a crucial step. The Red Team meticulously checks that all instructions have been followed, required sections are complete, and that every response aligns with the RFP's specific evaluation criteria. This includes verifying adherence to page limits, font and formatting requirements, and whether all requested attachments, past performance information, and certifications have been properly included.

Beyond compliance, the Red Team assesses the proposal's clarity, persuasiveness, and overall effectiveness in communicating the company's value proposition. A compliant proposal alone will not secure a contract; the document must also be compelling, customer-focused, and strategically positioned to differentiate the company from competitors. The Red Team carefully reviews the win themes, executive summary, and technical solution to ensure that the proposal clearly answers the government's needs while highlighting why the company is the best choice. This review process involves examining whether the document speaks directly to the agency's priorities, mission objectives, and hot-button issues, which were identified earlier in the Capture Management and Blue Team Process.

To further refine the proposal, the Red Team also evaluates its readability and logical flow. Government evaluators often review dozens, if not hundreds, of proposals, meaning a clear, well-structured, and easy-to-read submission will stand out. The Red Team provides feedback on whether sections are overly technical, redundant, or difficult to understand, making recommendations to simplify language while maintaining technical and compliance accuracy. The goal is to craft a proposal that is not only technically strong but also engaging and persuasive.

Another critical element of the Red Team's role is performing a competitive analysis review. Since multiple companies are bidding for the same contract, the Red Team's job is to determine whether the proposal effectively demonstrates a stronger solution than potential competitors. The team compares the company's strengths, pricing strategy, technical approach, and past performance to known or likely competitors in the space. If gaps are found in the differentiation strategy, the Red Team provides guidance on how to better highlight unique capabilities, proprietary methods, cost efficiency, innovation, or superior risk mitigation strategies that set the company apart.

The Red Team Process is structured as a formal review session, where team members provide detailed comments, recommendations, and evaluations using the same scoring system and methodology that the government will use during its review. The team scores the proposal against the evaluation factors outlined in the RFP, identifying strengths and weaknesses in technical approach, management plan, pricing, and past performance. If any section receives low marks or is deemed non-compliant, the Proposal Team is given clear instructions on what must be revised before finalization.

Following the Red Team review, the Proposal Team integrates all feedback and refines the document before it undergoes Gold Team review, the executive-level final sign-off process. The final version must be polished, fully compliant, strategically aligned, and persuasive, incorporating the critical insights gained from the Red Team review.

By applying the Red Team Process rigorously, companies significantly increase their win probability (Pwin) by ensuring that their proposal is not only compliant but also the strongest possible representation of their capabilities and value proposition. This process reduces the risk of losing on technicalities, ensures maximum scoring potential, and strengthens the company's position in competitive government contracting environments. Through this structured review process, companies can confidently submit proposals that stand out, win contracts, and establish long-term success in the federal marketplace.

The **Red Team** follows with a rigorous review, simulating the government evaluator's perspective. Composed of individuals not directly involved in writing the proposal, the Red Team critically assesses the bid's strengths, weaknesses, and competitive positioning. They provide recommendations on how to enhance the clarity of the executive summary, technical approach, management plan, and pricing strategy.

THE SHIPLEY ASSOCIATES GREEN TEAM PROCESS: OPTIMIZING PRICING FOR COMPETITIVE AND PROFITABLE GOVERNMENT PROPOSALS

The **Green Team**, responsible for pricing analysis, ensures that the financial structure of the proposal aligns with government expectations and competitor benchmarks. Their goal is to optimize cost-effectiveness while maintaining profitability.

The Green Team Process is a critical step in Shipley Associates' proposal development methodology, focused entirely on pricing strategy and cost optimization. Unlike other color teams, which review the technical, management, and compliance aspects of the proposal, the Green Team is solely responsible for ensuring that the financial components of the bid are structured for competitiveness, sustainability, and profitability. In federal contracting, a strong technical solution is not enough—pricing plays a decisive role in whether a proposal is awarded or rejected. A well-executed Green Team review ensures that the company submits a price that aligns with the government's expectations while remaining financially viable and defensible.

The primary goal of the Green Team is to develop a pricing strategy that balances cost-effectiveness with profitability. This requires an in-depth understanding of the agency's budget constraints, market conditions, and competitor pricing trends. The team analyzes historical contract data, procurement spending patterns, and cost realism expectations to determine an optimal pricing model. If the proposal is priced too high, the bid may be deemed non-competitive and lose to lower-cost competitors. If the proposal is priced too low, the government may question whether the contractor can perform the work effectively without financial risk, leading to concerns about underbidding or non-compliance with cost regulations. The Green Team ensures that pricing is both competitive and realistic, mitigating risks while maximizing the company's financial position.

The Green Team process begins with a thorough review of cost elements and pricing structures. Government contracts often require detailed cost breakdowns, including direct costs, indirect costs, labor rates, material expenses, subcontracting costs, overhead, and profit margins. The Green Team ensures that these components are accurately calculated, documented, and justified according to the contract type. Different types of government contracts, such as Firm-Fixed Price (FFP), Cost-Plus, Time and Materials (T&M), and Indefinite Delivery/Indefinite Quantity (IDIQ), each require different pricing methodologies, and the Green Team tailors its approach accordingly. For example, an FFP contract requires precise cost estimation and risk management, whereas a Cost-Plus contract allows for reimbursement of allowable expenses but requires stringent documentation. The Green Team ensures that the company's pricing model aligns with the contract type and regulatory requirements outlined in the Federal Acquisition Regulation (FAR) and the Defense Federal Acquisition Regulation Supplement (DFARS).

Another key function of the Green Team is competitive price benchmarking. Since government contracts are awarded based on best value trade-offs, where both price and technical capability are evaluated, the Green Team conducts market research and competitive analysis to understand how rival firms are likely to bid. The team reviews publicly available procurement data from sources like SAM.gov, the Federal Procurement Data System (FPDS), and agency spending forecasts to identify past contract awards and the pricing trends of competing firms. Using competitive intelligence, the Green Team refines the company's pricing strategy to ensure that it is neither underpriced nor overpriced compared to market expectations.

Cost realism is a critical factor in government proposals, and the Green Team ensures that every pricing component is defensible and justified. Government agencies evaluate whether proposed costs are realistic for the work to be performed, reflect a clear understanding of the contract requirements, and are consistent with industry standards. If a proposal contains unreasonably low labor rates, unrealistic direct costs, or unsubstantiated pricing assumptions, it may be deemed non-compliant. The Green Team reviews labor category mappings, cost estimation methodologies, and escalation factors to ensure that the company's pricing is both competitive and justifiable.

The Green Team also evaluates subcontractor pricing and cost allocations, ensuring that subcontracted work is priced appropriately and does not create financial risks. Government contracts often require subcontracting plans, particularly for small business participation, and the Green Team ensures that the cost structure accounts for these obligations. If subcontractor pricing is too high, it can reduce the overall competitiveness of the bid. If it's too low, it could result in execution challenges or compliance violations. The Green Team works closely with finance, procurement, and operations teams to verify that subcontractor costs are reasonable and that they align with the prime contractor's financial strategy.

Risk mitigation is a key focus of the Green Team review, as improper pricing can lead to financial losses, contract performance issues, or even bid protests from competing firms. The Green Team conducts sensitivity analyses and risk assessments to evaluate the impact of cost fluctuations, wage increases, material shortages, and regulatory compliance costs. By identifying financial risks in advance, the Green Team helps create contingency plans and ensures that the pricing model remains resilient under changing market conditions.

Once the Green Team has completed its detailed pricing analysis, it presents its findings and recommendations to senior leadership during the Gold Team review, which is the final executive decision-making process before submission. The Gold Team evaluates whether the proposal, as a whole, is a strong business case, while the Green Team's focus remains on ensuring that the cost structure supports both competitiveness and profitability. If necessary, adjustments are made to optimize the profit margin, indirect cost allocations, and resource distribution before the final pricing submission.

The Green Team Process is an essential component of Shipley Associates' methodology because pricing is often the deciding factor in competitive government bids. Companies that fail to implement a rigorous Green Team review risk submitting uncompetitive or unrealistic pricing, leading to lost contract opportunities or performance challenges. By leveraging historical data, market intelligence, and strategic cost modeling, the Green Team ensures that the company submits a proposal that meets the government's pricing expectations while maximizing financial sustainability. A well-executed Green Team process directly contributes to higher win rates, increased profitability, and long-term success in government contracting.

THE SHIPLEY ASSOCIATES GOLD TEAM PROCESS: THE FINAL EXECUTIVE REVIEW AND BUSINESS DECISION FOR SUBMISSION

After incorporating Red Team feedback, the Gold Team, made up of senior leadership and capture executives, conducts a final executive review. This team ensures that the pricing strategy is competitive and that the overall bid represents a strong business case. They confirm risk mitigation strategies, team qualifications, and value propositions before approving the final submission.

The Gold Team Process serves as the ultimate executive review, marking the final stage in the Shipley Associates proposal development lifecycle. While the Red Team ensures the proposal is compliant and compelling from an evaluator's perspective, the Gold Team provides a high-level business review, focusing on financial, operational, and strategic viability. This team is comprised of senior executives, capture managers, financial officers, and business decision-makers, ensuring that the bid represents a strong business case, aligns with corporate objectives, and presents an optimized pricing strategy with acceptable risk.

The Gold Team's role is crucial because it determines whether the company should move forward with the submission. The government contracting process is highly competitive, and submitting a proposal is a significant investment of time, resources, and personnel. If a bid is submitted without a realistic probability of win (Pwin) or without a sound financial structure, it can result in wasted resources, poor profitability, or even performance risks if awarded. The Gold Team's review acts as the final checkpoint, ensuring that every aspect of the bid is strategically aligned, financially viable, and operationally feasible.

The Gold Team begins its review by analyzing the proposal from a business risk perspective. A government contract may appear lucrative, but it can introduce unforeseen cost burdens, liability, and compliance risks that could impact long-term profitability. The team examines contract terms and conditions, risk mitigation strategies, and past performance factors to determine whether the opportunity aligns with the company's financial health and risk tolerance. This assessment is particularly important for small and mid-sized businesses that may not have the financial or operational bandwidth to absorb potential losses or contract modifications.

Pricing is one of the most critical elements evaluated during the Gold Team Review. Government agencies assess bids based on a best value tradeoff, balancing cost with technical capability. If the price is too high, the bid may be deemed uncompetitive; if it's too low, it may raise concerns about the company's ability to deliver quality performance. The Gold Team ensures that the pricing structure is competitive while still allowing for profitability, operational sustainability, and risk absorption. They analyze direct and indirect costs, subcontractor pricing, escalation factors, and cost realism to ensure that the proposal's pricing aligns with industry benchmarks.

Beyond pricing, the Gold Team scrutinizes the value proposition and overall strength of the bid. Every government contract evaluation considers technical expertise, past performance, management approach, and cost-effectiveness. The Gold Team assesses whether the proposal effectively communicates the company's key differentiators, ensuring that the executive summary, technical volume, and management approach reinforce the company's ability to deliver superior value. They evaluate win themes, key personnel qualifications, past performance narratives, and subcontracting relationships to confirm that the bid presents a strong and credible business case.

Risk mitigation is another fundamental focus of the Gold Team Process. Government contracts often involve stringent compliance requirements, performance milestones, and financial penalties for delays or non-compliance. The Gold Team examines contingency plans, risk registers, compliance matrices, and quality control measures to ensure that every identified risk has a corresponding mitigation strategy. This step is particularly important when bidding for cost-plus, fixed-price, or indefinite-delivery/indefinite-quantity (IDIQ) contracts, where financial and performance risks vary significantly.

The Gold Team review also involves a final executive decision on bid/no-bid for submission. While previous color team reviews (such as Red Team and Black Team) focus on the strength of the proposal's technical and competitive aspects, the Gold Team makes a holistic business decision. If the bid presents too much financial risk, if the pricing is not competitive, or if the company's capacity to execute is uncertain, the Gold Team has the authority to halt the submission. If approved, the final bid is locked, reviewed for last-minute compliance checks, and prepared for submission.

Once the Gold Team approves the bid, the company submits the final proposal package, ensuring that all electronic and hard-copy submission requirements are met. This includes checking SAM.gov registrations, ensuring that required certifications are included, and meeting all electronic submission protocols as dictated by the government agency. The Gold Team signs off on the proposal, ensuring full corporate endorsement before submission.

The Shipley Associates Gold Team Process is an essential final step in government contracting, ensuring that each bid is financially viable, strategically aligned, and operationally executable. Companies that implement a rigorous Gold Team Review significantly improve their chances of winning contracts without exposing themselves to unnecessary financial or operational risks. The Gold Team process is more than just a formality—it is the critical business decision point that determines whether a company will move forward with confidence in its ability to win and execute a government contract successfully.

THE SHIPLEY ASSOCIATES BLACK TEAM PROCESS: UNDERSTANDING THE COMPETITION AND PREEMPTIVELY COUNTERING THEIR STRATEGIES

Post-Bid Activities and Contract Fulfillment

In government contracting, understanding the competition is just as important as understanding the requirements of the contract itself. This is where the Shipley Associates Black Team Process plays a critical role. While much of the capture and proposal process focuses on developing a compliant, compelling, and persuasive proposal, the Black Team's mission is to analyze, anticipate, and neutralize the competition before the proposal is even submitted. This process ensures that the company's submission is not only strong but also positioned to outperform every competitor in the field.

The Black Team operates as a simulated competitor analysis unit, structured to think and act like the company's strongest rivals in the bidding process. It consists of internal subject matter experts, business development professionals, and external consultants with experience in competitive bidding and procurement strategies. These team members are tasked with assessing the strengths, weaknesses, opportunities, and threats (SWOT) posed by other firms likely to bid on the same opportunity. Their primary focus is to identify what advantages competitors have, how they will likely position themselves, and what countermeasures must be taken to ensure that the company's proposal is stronger, more aligned with the government's needs, and ultimately more likely to win.

The first phase of the Black Team's work begins with deep competitor research. This involves analyzing the government agency's procurement history, evaluating previous contract awards, and identifying which firms have historically competed for similar contracts. By reviewing the size, capabilities, past performance, and differentiators of likely competitors, the Black Team can predict their bid strategies and uncover potential weaknesses that can be exploited. They look at how competitors price their services, what technical approaches they favor, and where they may have gaps in compliance or execution. This research often includes a thorough review of publicly available information, such as Federal Procurement Data System (FPDS) records, contractor past performance databases, industry news, and analyst reports.

Once the competitive intelligence has been gathered, the Black Team shifts into the strategic role-playing phase, often referred to as a "Black Hat Review." In this exercise, Black Team members assume the identities of major competitors, adopting their business models, strengths, and proposal strategies. They analyze how these competitors are likely to position their bids, what price points they may offer, how they will highlight their past performance, and what their potential weak points are. By conducting this exercise, the Black Team creates a realistic and predictive model of the competition, allowing the company to prepare counterstrategies in its proposal.

The findings of the Black Team directly impact the Capture Plan and Proposal Strategy, ensuring that the company does not simply submit a good proposal, but one that is designed to outscore and outperform the competition. If, for example, a competitor is known for being the lowest-cost bidder, the Black Team may recommend refining the company's value-based pricing strategy, ensuring that cost is balanced with superior risk mitigation, innovation, and long-term sustainability. If a competitor has an established relationship with the contracting agency, the Black Team may suggest leveraging key personnel, emphasizing customer intimacy, or demonstrating how past performance exceeds that of competitors.

Throughout this process, the Black Team works closely with the Capture Manager, Blue Team, and Proposal Team to adjust the overall proposal messaging, pricing, and technical solution based on the anticipated competition. Their work ensures that the company is proactively positioning itself ahead of rivals, rather than simply reacting to the government's requirements.

The final phase of the Black Team's process involves a comprehensive debrief and strategy refinement session. This is where the team presents their findings, competitor strategies, potential threats, and recommended solutions to the Capture Manager and senior executives. The company's Proposal Strategy is adjusted accordingly, incorporating tactics that specifically counter competitor strengths while reinforcing the company's unique selling points.

By integrating the Black Team Process into Capture Management, the company ensures that it is not just meeting the minimum requirements of the contract but is winning based on a well-researched, strategic, and competitive approach. The Black Team helps uncover hidden risks, exposes weaknesses in competitors, and provides the insight needed to gain a significant edge in government contracting. In an industry where every point in an evaluation matters, a strong Black Team process can mean the difference between securing a multimillion-dollar contract or losing to a better-prepared competitor. This level of competitor intelligence and strategic positioning is essential for companies looking to establish long-term success in federal contracting.

Once the proposal is submitted, Black Team reviews are conducted internally to identify lessons learned, regardless of the bid outcome. If the company wins the contract, this team evaluates execution risks, transition plans, and contract compliance measures. If the bid is lost, the Black Team conducts a post-mortem analysis, gathering customer feedback to improve future proposals.

Following award, contract execution begins with seamless transition planning, compliance tracking, and performance monitoring. A strong post-bid strategy includes establishing a relationship with agency contract officers, ensuring deliverables are met on time, and positioning the company for future opportunities.

Summary

By integrating the **Shipley Associates Color Team Process** into Capture Management, Proposal Development, and Post-Bid Activities, businesses can maximize their win potential. The White and Blue Teams ensure early positioning and customer engagement, the Pink, Red, Gold, and Green Teams refine proposal quality, and the Black Team ensures continuous improvement. This structured approach transforms government contracting from a reactive bidding process into a proactive strategy that builds long-term success.

CHAPTER 3

WHAT IS CAPTURE MANAGEMENT?

Assessing Opportunities with Precision

Capture management is the cornerstone of Nijsha Enterprise Inc.'s strategic approach to securing government contracts. By systematically assessing opportunities, aligning resources, and executing both pre-bid and post-bid activities with precision, we increase our probability of success in the competitive government contracting space. Capture management begins with a **rigorous opportunity assessment**. We meticulously evaluate each potential contract to ensure alignment with our core competencies, past performance, and strategic growth objectives. This process includes analyzing **agency needs, funding allocations, competitive landscapes, and customer pain points** —a level of due diligence that prevents wasted effort on low-probability pursuits and focuses our energy on contracts where we are positioned to succeed.

The foundation of successful contract acquisition lies in identifying the right opportunities. We leverage data analytics, industry trends, and government procurement forecasts to determine which solicitations align with our capabilities and long-term business goals. Through a structured capture management process, we evaluate contract viability based on compliance requirements, competition analysis, and strategic fit. This ensures that we pursue opportunities with the highest probability of success while maintaining a sustainable pipeline of contracts.

The Strategic Imperative of Capture Management at Nijsha Enterprise Inc.

At Nijsha Enterprise Inc., we recognize that success in government contracting is not left to chance. It is the result of a disciplined, systematic approach known as **Capture Management**—a methodology that allows us to assess opportunities, allocate resources effectively, and execute winning strategies from the earliest stages of the bidding process to post-award contract fulfillment.

Assigning Resources for Maximum Impact

Once a viable opportunity is identified, we strategically assign the necessary personnel and technical resources to **maximize our competitive advantage**. This involves mobilizing subject matter experts, pricing strategists, proposal writers, and compliance specialists—ensuring that every aspect of our response meets or exceeds federal expectations. Our ability to efficiently allocate resources strengthens our responsiveness and ability to develop compelling solutions tailored to government requirements.

Assigning the right personnel and financial resources becomes critical. Nijsha Enterprise Inc. strategically allocates subject matter experts, proposal managers, pricing analysts, and technical writers to ensure the development of a compelling and compliant proposal. Additionally, we engage with teaming partners and subcontractors when necessary to enhance our capabilities and meet contract requirements.

Executing Pre-Bid Activities with Tactical Precision

Pre-bid activities define the foundation of a successful capture strategy. At Nijsha Enterprise Inc., we leverage **market intelligence, customer engagement, and competitive positioning** to refine our approach.

Our pre-bid process focuses on proactive engagement with government agencies, refining our understanding of their mission needs and pain points. Through capability briefings, agency relationship-building, and intelligence gathering, we position Nijsha as a trusted solutions provider before the solicitation is even released. Additionally, we conduct detailed competitor analyses and price-to-win assessments to develop a strong competitive advantage.

We also place a high emphasis on internal collaboration. Before a proposal is even drafted, our capture team ensures that our pricing strategy, technical approach, and compliance measures are fully aligned with government expectations. Internal reviews, such as Pink Team and Red Team evaluations, allow us to refine our messaging and ensure that the final proposal submission meets the highest standards.

Our approach includes:

- Conducting **stakeholder outreach** to understand key decision-makers and their priorities.
- Engaging in **early business development discussions** to shape requirements before the solicitation is finalized.
- **Crafting a win strategy** that differentiates us from competitors and emphasizes our unique value proposition.
- Conducting **pricing-to-win analysis** to ensure cost-effectiveness while maintaining profitability.

This phase is critical because it positions us to respond **proactively, rather than reactively**, when the official solicitation is released.

Executing a World-Class Proposal Strategy

With a well-defined capture plan, we transition into proposal development. Our proposal process is structured, disciplined, and driven by **compliance, clarity, and compelling storytelling**. We integrate:

- **Technical excellence** to demonstrate our solution capabilities.
- **Management approach** to showcase our ability to execute successfully.
- **Pricing strategy** to balance competitiveness with profitability.
- **Compliance rigor** to ensure adherence to federal acquisition regulations.

Additionally, **internal reviews, Red Team assessments, and executive oversight** ensure our proposal stands out in a highly competitive landscape.

Post-Bid Execution: Turning Wins into Lasting Success

Winning a contract is only the beginning. Our **post-bid activities focus on flawless execution, contract compliance, and relationship management**.

Submitting a proposal is not the end of the process—securing the contract requires a strong post-bid strategy. Nijsha Enterprise Inc. actively engages in bid reviews, negotiations, and presentations to reinforce our competitive edge. We anticipate government clarifications and prepare responsive, data-driven answers to any inquiries. If awarded the contract, our transition and execution plans are immediately set in motion to ensure compliance, performance excellence, and long-term contract sustainability.

By maintaining a disciplined capture management process, Nijsha Enterprise Inc. continues to expand its presence in federal contracting. We remain committed to innovation, efficiency, and strategic growth, ensuring that every contract pursued is positioned for success.

We ensure:

- A **smooth transition from capture to contract management** through well-documented handoff processes.
- **Consistent communication with contracting officers** to proactively address any concerns.
- **Performance monitoring and quality assurance** to meet or exceed deliverable expectations.
- **Pursuit of follow-on opportunities** by continuously adding value beyond the initial contract scope.

Our reputation is built not just on **winning contracts but on delivering results** that lead to **repeat business, contract renewals, and expansion into new opportunities**.

THE REALM OF FEDERAL CONTRACTING

In the realm of federal contracting, a robust capture management process is pivotal for enhancing the probability of securing contracts. This process involves a series of strategic steps executed from the moment a company decides to pursue a government contract until the request for proposal (RFP) is released. Here's how a typical company employs capture management techniques:

1. Opportunity Identification and Assessment: The process begins with diligent market research and leveraging existing networks to identify potential government contracts. This step often involves the use of CRM systems (e.g., Salesforce, GovWin) to track opportunities and gather relevant data. Companies evaluate these opportunities based on their alignment with strategic goals, capabilities, and resource availability.

The initial phase of capture management—Opportunity Identification and Assessment—is pivotal for companies aiming to secure government contracts. This stage sets the foundation for all subsequent capture activities, emphasizing the importance of meticulous market research and the strategic use of existing networks to uncover potential opportunities.

Market Research: Market research is an extensive process where companies analyze public sector demands to identify upcoming projects and potential government needs that align with their service offerings. This research goes beyond mere identification; it involves a detailed examination of forecasted government spending, review of past RFPs, and insights into budget allocations for specific agencies.

This allows companies to anticipate the type of contracts that may be put out to tender, understanding the scope and scale that align with their operational strengths and business objectives.

Leveraging Existing Networks: Utilizing established networks is crucial in the government contracting realm. These networks could consist of prior government clients, partners in joint ventures, or even contacts within industry associations. Networking helps in gaining insider knowledge about unannounced projects or changes in procurement strategy that are not publicly available. Engaging with these networks allows companies to position themselves favorably early in the decision-making process, potentially influencing project specifications to match their capabilities.

Utilization of CRM Systems: Customer Relationship Management (CRM) systems like Salesforce or GovWin play a critical role in tracking and managing government contracting opportunities. These systems serve as repositories of valuable data on potential and current clients, past interactions, and historical contract details. By analyzing this data, companies can identify patterns, tailor their marketing strategies, and align their business development efforts more closely with government requirements. These platforms often provide tools for tracking communications, setting reminders for follow-up actions, and scheduling meetings, which are essential for maintaining active engagement with key stakeholders.

Evaluation of Opportunities: Once potential contracts are identified, the next step involves a thorough evaluation based on several criteria:

Strategic Alignment: Assessing whether an opportunity aligns with the company's long-term strategic goals. This includes considering whether the contract would help the company enter new markets, strengthen existing capabilities, or enhance its reputation in a specific field.

Capability Match: Determining if the company has the necessary technical expertise, resources, and technology to deliver the project requirements effectively. This often involves a gap analysis to identify any needs for additional resources or partnerships.

Resource Availability: Examining current resource allocation and availability, including personnel, technology, and financial resources. This ensures that the company can meet the contract demands without overextending its existing commitments.

Decision to Pursue: Based on the comprehensive analysis, a decision is made whether to pursue the opportunity. This decision is typically supported by a cost-benefit analysis, weighing the potential return on investment against the cost of proposal development and project execution. Only opportunities that meet a predefined threshold for profitability and strategic fit are moved forward in the capture process.

By systematically executing the Opportunity Identification and Assessment phase, companies can ensure that they focus their efforts on the most promising government contracts, thereby optimizing their resources and enhancing their chances of successful capture. This strategic approach not only streamlines the capture process but also aligns it closely with corporate objectives, driving growth and profitability in the competitive government contracting landscape.

2. Customer Relationship Building: Establishing and maintaining strong relationships with potential and current government clients is crucial. Capture managers engage in continuous dialogue with key decision-makers and stakeholders to understand their needs, challenges, and preferences, which helps in tailoring solutions accordingly.

3. Competitive Analysis and Positioning: A thorough competitive analysis helps identify primary competitors and assess their strengths and weaknesses relative to the company's capabilities. Tools like Black Hat reviews are used to predict competitors' strategies and develop effective counterstrategies, refining the company's unique selling propositions.

Competitive analysis is an essential component of any company's strategy to secure government contracts. It involves a thorough investigation into the capabilities and strategies of primary competitors. This analysis allows companies to gauge their own strengths and weaknesses relative to the market and adapt their strategies to better align with the demands of potential contracts. Tools such as Black Hat reviews are instrumental in this phase, helping predict and counteract competitors' tactics and refine the company's unique selling propositions.

However, while the structured approaches proposed by methodologies like Shipley's are invaluable, they may not always be feasible or entirely suitable for every company. For instance, a firm might need to adapt the rigorous processes to fit its unique context or constraints. This might involve modifying standard procedures to better align with the company's size, resource availability, or specific market conditions.

In adapting these methodologies, it's crucial for companies to develop a brand opportunity assessment that effectively captures and analyzes market data to inform their strategies. This approach entails not only understanding the competitive landscape but also building robust customer relationship management practices. Successful customer relationship management involves continuous interaction with potential clients to understand their needs and adjust offerings accordingly, which is vital for crafting proposals that resonate with government agencies.

For many companies, finding the right mix of tools and techniques is key to developing effective strategies. As Michael E. Porter famously said, "The essence of strategy is choosing what not to do." This quote highlights the importance of discernment in strategy development—choosing not just what tactics to employ but also what to omit based on the company's specific context and goals.

Companies are encouraged to explore and integrate various strategic tools and approaches described in this guide, tailoring them to their unique needs. This might mean combining elements of Shipley's structured methodologies with customized tools or alternative strategies that better suit the specific challenges and opportunities they face in the government contracting landscape.

By embracing a flexible approach to competitive analysis and strategy formulation, companies can enhance their responsiveness to RFPs, improve their competitive edge, and increase their success rates in securing government contracts. This tailored approach ensures that strategies are not only theoretically sound but also practically applicable, leading to better alignment with both corporate objectives and market realities.

4. *Internal Team Collaboration*: Cross-functional collaboration is essential, involving teams from business development, technical fields, finance, and other relevant departments. These teams work under the leadership of the capture manager to ensure that proposals are technically sound and strategically aligned with the client's goals.

Effective internal team collaboration is a cornerstone of successful capture management and proposal development. In the complex arena of government contracting, where technical soundness and strategic alignment are paramount, the synergy between various departmental teams becomes critical. This collaboration often extends beyond the internal framework of a company, embracing the mentorship from more established, experienced entities within the industry.

The Role of Cross-Functional Teams:

Cross-functional teams in a company typically include professionals from business development, technical fields, finance, and other departments relevant to the contracting process. These teams, led by a capture manager, are tasked with ensuring that every aspect of a proposal aligns perfectly with both the client's specifications and the company's capabilities. The integration of diverse perspectives not only enhances the proposal's quality but also ensures a comprehensive approach to problem-solving and strategy development.

Expanding Collaboration through Mentor-Protege Programs:

To further strengthen their position and capabilities, companies, especially newer and smaller firms, can benefit immensely from participating in Mentor-Protege Programs. These programs are designed to help less experienced companies (proteges) gain the necessary insights and capabilities through the guidance of more established firms (mentors) in the industry. For instance, the Small Business Administration (SBA) offers a Mentor-Protege Program that encourages larger, more experienced businesses to assist smaller businesses in enhancing their ability to compete for federal contracts.

Mentors provide a range of support, including technical and management assistance, financial assistance in the form of equity investments or loans, subcontract support, and assistance in performing prime contracts through joint venture arrangements, ensuring a higher chance of securing and successfully executing government contracts.

Nijsha Enterprise, Inc. as a Mentor:

Nijsha Enterprise, Inc., with its wealth of experience and established success in the federal business space, is committed to leveraging its resources and knowledge base to mentor emerging companies. This mentorship can be incredibly beneficial for new entrants into the government contracting world, who can learn from Nijsha's insights on navigating the complex federal procurement process, developing competitive proposals, and managing government contracts effectively.

Example of Effective Mentorship:

An exemplary case of successful mentorship can be seen where a well-established defense contractor guided a small tech startup through the intricacies of a highly technical RFP, leading to a joint venture that won the startup its first major federal contract. This partnership not only provided the startup with essential hands-on experience but also established a foundation for future success in the industry.

Encouragement for Emerging Contractors:

For emerging contractors, the opportunity to collaborate with a mentor like Nijsha Enterprise, Inc. is invaluable. These partnerships can demystify the process of federal contracting, accelerate learning curves, and provide the necessary exposure to industry best practices. By embracing the mentor-protege model, new companies are not just surviving; they are positioned to thrive and excel in the competitive federal contracting arena.

Internal team collaboration enriched with external mentorship creates a powerful synergy that can dramatically improve a company's prospects in government contracting. For companies like Nijsha Enterprise, Inc., participating in mentor-protege programs is not just about business growth but also about fostering a vibrant, competitive, and capable industry ecosystem. Through such collaborative and mentorship-driven approaches, the pathway to success in federal contracting becomes more accessible, informed, and strategically sound.

At Nijsha Enterprise Inc., capture management is not an isolated function—it is **embedded in our DNA**. Every contract we pursue is backed by strategic analysis, expert execution, and an unwavering commitment to **delivering excellence in federal contracting**.

Through disciplined capture management, we **turn opportunities into contracts, and contracts into long-term partnerships**. This relentless pursuit of excellence is what distinguishes us as a premier government contractor in an increasingly competitive marketplace.

5. Solution Development and Validation: Tailored solutions that address specific needs and hot buttons of the government client are crafted through brainstorming sessions and solution design meetings. These solutions are validated through customer feedback and internal reviews to ensure compliance and effectiveness.

In the competitive landscape of government contracting, developing and validating solutions that precisely meet the client's needs is not just beneficial—it's essential. This approach hinges on a deep understanding of the customer's goals, challenges, and what genuinely matters to their operations, often termed as understanding "what keeps the customer up at night." For companies like Nijsha Enterprise, mastering this understanding has been a cornerstone of their strategy, enabling them to deliver tailored solutions that resonate deeply with their clients and consistently result in contract awards.

Gathering Customer Knowledge:

The first step in solution development and validation involves an immersive process of gathering detailed knowledge about the customer. This is not limited to the specifications listed in the RFP but extends to gaining a nuanced understanding of the customer's broader strategic objectives and day-to-day challenges. Techniques used include engaging with the customer through formal and informal communications, participating in industry events where customers discuss their pain points, and utilizing advanced market research tools that provide insights into government agencies' operational hurdles.

Customer intimacy and a deep understanding of customer needs play a pivotal role in evaluating and securing government contract opportunities. By building strong relationships and comprehensively analyzing customer requirements, companies can align their capabilities with the specific needs of government agencies. This process, as outlined in the attached slide deck, involves multiple stages within capture management, pipeline development, pricing, solutions development, and proposal preparation. Each phase is essential in increasing the probability of winning a contract and ensuring long-term success.

To evaluate opportunities effectively, businesses must first gather and organize intelligence about their target agencies. This includes understanding procurement trends, historical purchases, agency pain points, and funding availability. Developing relationships with key stakeholders within the agency is crucial. Engaging with program managers, contracting officers, and end-users allows businesses to gain insights into project priorities and technical expectations. Customer engagement must begin well before the release of a Request for Proposal (RFP), as early conversations shape requirements and influence procurement strategies.

The next phase is opportunity analysis, where competitive intelligence and internal capability assessments determine the feasibility of pursuing a contract. This includes a thorough gap analysis—identifying strengths, weaknesses, opportunities, and threats (SWOT). The slide deck highlights how organizations should conduct a Probability of Win (P-Win) analysis, using best practices rather than common, reactionary methods. A structured approach ensures that efforts are focused on high-value, winnable contracts rather than expending resources on opportunities that do not align with company strengths.

Developing a win strategy is essential in positioning a company effectively against competitors. This includes aligning pricing strategies with procurement models such as Firm-Fixed Price (FFP), Cost-Plus (CPIF, CPFF), or Time and Materials (T&M). The customer's evaluation model, whether based on Best Value or Lowest Price Technically Acceptable (LPTA), dictates how a proposal should be structured. Gaming the pricing approach—understanding how competitors will price their bids and how the customer perceives value—is critical in crafting a compelling offer.

Capture planning follows the development of a win strategy. The capture lifecycle involves an iterative process where solutions are validated, teams are formed, and customer feedback is incorporated into the approach. Teaming arrangements, including subcontracting and small business partnerships, are vital in meeting government contract set-asides and satisfying agency diversity requirements. The ability to present a well-organized, risk-mitigated, and technically superior solution is what sets successful contractors apart.

Proposal preparation is the culmination of capture management efforts. The proposal development team, consisting of business development leads, program managers, technical leads, cost estimators, and subcontract managers, works collaboratively to craft a compliant and persuasive submission. The slide deck outlines the importance of section reviews such as Pink Team (internally focused reviews) and Red Team (external competitive assessments). A well-executed review process ensures that technical solutions are validated, pricing is competitive, and the narrative resonates with evaluators.

Post-bid activities are just as critical as pre-bid preparation. The Post-Bid Phase includes negotiations, contract formation, and contract fulfillment. After submission, companies must be prepared for clarification questions, oral presentations, and further pricing discussions. Once awarded, contract execution must be seamless, with careful attention to performance management, risk mitigation, and customer satisfaction.

The transition plan must ensure that deliverables are met efficiently, maintaining compliance with all contractual obligations.

Using these methodologies ensures a structured and disciplined approach to winning government contracts. Organizations that invest in capture management processes improve their ability to anticipate customer needs, align their solutions with funding priorities, and outmaneuver competitors. Rather than reacting to RFP releases, proactive capture strategies enable companies to shape requirements, influence procurement decisions, and secure long-term agency relationships. Ultimately, government contracting is not about a single bid—it is about establishing a reputation for reliability, quality, and value that leads to sustained business growth.

Developing Tailored Solutions:

With a robust foundation of customer knowledge, Nijsha Enterprise engages in comprehensive brainstorming sessions and solution design meetings, aiming to address not just the explicit needs but also the implicit expectations of the government client. These sessions involve cross-functional teams from technical, management, finance, and operational departments to ensure that every aspect of the solution is integrated and aligned with the client's goals.

The emphasis is on creating innovative solutions that not only solve the problem at hand but also offer added value—whether through cost savings, improved efficiency, or enhanced effectiveness. For instance, if the customer is concerned about cybersecurity threats, Nijsha doesn't just propose a standard security package. Instead, they offer a custom solution that integrates cutting-edge technology with training and support, ensuring that the client's staff is well-prepared to handle potential threats.

Validating Solutions Through Customer Feedback:

Validation is a critical step in the solution development process. Nijsha actively seeks customer feedback to ensure that the proposed solutions truly resonate with the client's needs and address their concerns. This feedback is gathered through presentations, prototype demonstrations, or pilot projects, depending on the nature of the solution and the client's openness to engagement during the proposal phase.

Mastering What Keeps the Customer Up at Night:

Understanding and addressing what keeps the customer up at night involves delving into the deeper, sometimes unspoken concerns that affect the client's operations. Nijsha's approach is to make these concerns the focal point of their solution development. For example, if a client is worried about the sustainability and environmental impact of their operations, Nijsha's proposal will highlight eco-friendly technologies and practices, demonstrating a commitment to not just meeting but exceeding the government's sustainability goals.

Tailored Solutions That Matter:

The effectiveness of this approach has been proven time and again through successful contract awards. By tailoring solutions that directly impact and improve the client's operational capability, Nijsha has positioned itself as a partner that understands and prioritizes the client's needs. This customer-centric approach not only leads to immediate contract wins but also builds long-term relationships and a strong reputation in the industry.

Implementing a customer-centric strategy in your business model, akin to the practices used by successful government contractors like Nijsha Enterprise, involves a multi-step approach focused on deeply understanding and addressing the specific needs of your clients. Here's how you can incorporate these strategies into your business to enhance your chances of securing contracts and building enduring customer relationships:

A. Conduct Thorough Market and Customer Research:

Start by gathering as much information as possible about your potential clients and the market landscape. This involves:

- **Industry Analysis:** Understand the broader industry trends, challenges, and opportunities. Use resources like industry reports, market analysis papers, and seminars.
- **Direct Engagement:** Participate in industry forums, workshops, and conferences where potential clients are likely to discuss their challenges and needs.
- **Customer Interaction:** Engage directly with potential clients through meetings, casual conversations, and formal needs-assessment sessions to gather detailed insights into their specific problems and aspirations.

B. Establish Robust Internal Collaboration:

Develop solutions that are integrated and comprehensive by fostering strong collaboration across your organization. This should include:

- **Cross-functional Teams:** Form teams that include members from technical, sales, finance, and operations to ensure all perspectives are considered in solution development.
- **Regular Brainstorming Sessions:** Conduct regular meetings to brainstorm solutions, with a focus on innovation and customization to meet client-specific needs.

C. **Develop Tailored Solutions:**

Use the insights gained from your research and internal collaboration to develop tailored solutions for your clients. Ensure that these solutions are:

- **Customized:** Design solutions that address not just the general needs but also the unique challenges and goals of each client.
- **Innovative:** Incorporate the latest technologies and practices that can offer additional value to your clients.
- **Scalable:** Ensure that the solutions can be scaled or adapted as per the changing needs of the client.

D. **Validate Solutions Through Client Feedback:**

Before finalizing your proposal, validate your solutions by:

- **Prototyping:** Where possible, develop prototypes or pilot programs to demonstrate the effectiveness of your solutions.
- **Feedback Loops:** Present your solutions to the clients and request feedback. Use this feedback to refine and adjust your proposals to better meet the client's expectations.

E. **Focus on the Client's Core Concerns:**

Make a concerted effort to understand and alleviate the client's primary concerns, whether they are operational, financial, or strategic. This involves:

- **Deep Dives:** Regularly engage with the client to get to the heart of their operational challenges.
- **Proactive Solutions:** Anticipate potential issues that the

client might face in the future and propose proactive solutions in your bids.

F. **Cultivate Long-term Relationships:**

Building and maintaining long-term relationships with clients goes beyond individual contracts.

This can be achieved by:

- **Consistent Communication:** Keep in touch with the client even after project completion to offer support and updates on new developments.
- **Continued Service Improvement:** Regularly update your service offerings based on feedback and changes in technology to keep your solutions relevant and competitive.

G. **Learn and Adapt:**

Finally, continuously learn from each engagement. Gather lessons learned and use this knowledge to refine your approach to future proposals and client engagements.

6. *Win Strategy Formulation*: With a deep understanding of the customer's needs and the competitive landscape, a clear win strategy is developed. This strategy covers technical solutions, pricing, risk management, and business approaches, documented in a comprehensive capture plan that guides all actions and is updated regularly.

Formulating a win strategy is a critical step in the process of securing government contracts. It encapsulates the culmination of a deep understanding of the client's needs, a keen awareness of the competitive landscape, and a robust alignment of your company's capabilities with the project requirements. Here's a detailed approach to developing and refining a win strategy:

A. **Comprehensive Customer Analysis:**

The foundation of an effective win strategy is a thorough understanding of the customer's needs. This involves not just the basic requirements outlined in the RFP but also the broader objectives and challenges the customer faces. Engage in direct communications, participate in pre-solicitation meetings, and use feedback from past projects to grasp what the customer truly values. This deep dive helps in identifying the critical pain points and priorities that your **proposal must address.**

B. **Competitive Landscape Assessment:**

Understanding your competition is as crucial as understanding your client. Conduct a detailed analysis of potential competitors, which includes reviewing their past performances, capabilities, and likely approaches to the contract. Tools like a SWOT analysis (Strengths, Weaknesses, Opportunities, Threats) can be invaluable here. Knowing the competition helps in positioning your proposal to highlight how your solutions are superior or more relevant to the client's needs.

C. **Strategic Alignment of Capabilities:**

Once you have a clear picture of what the client needs and what your competitors might offer, align your company's capabilities to these insights. This means ensuring that your proposal emphasizes your strengths that are most relevant to the RFP and showcases your ability to deliver better value than your competitors. For example, if the client values innovation in technology and you have a strong R&D department, highlight past innovations and propose a forward-thinking solution tailored to the client's operations.

D. **Pricing Strategy:**

Developing a competitive pricing strategy is a delicate balance between being attractive to the customer and remaining profitable. Utilize cost-benefit analysis to set a price that reflects the value of the solution and remains competitive in the market. Consider different pricing models like Fixed-Price, Cost-Reimbursement, or Time & Materials, based on what best suits the project scope and client expectations.

E. **Risk Management Plan:**

Identify potential risks associated with the project and propose mitigation strategies within the proposal. This not only increases the credibility of your bid but also demonstrates proactive thinking and planning. Risks can range from technical challenges, supply chain issues, to regulatory changes. Effective risk management shows that your company is prepared to handle uncertainties efficiently.

F. **Dynamic Documentation in the Capture Plan:**

Document all aspects of your win strategy in a detailed capture plan. This plan should include timelines, roles and responsibilities, resource allocation, and strategic milestones. Regularly update the capture plan to reflect any new insights or changes in the competitive landscape or customer requirements. This living document ensures that all team members are aligned and can adapt to changes swiftly.

G. **Regular Strategy Reviews and Updates:**

Win strategies should not be static. Hold regular review sessions to assess the relevance and effectiveness of the strategy against ongoing market and internal changes. These reviews can be part of scheduled strategy meetings or ad hoc as needed based on external changes like new competitor tactics or shifts in customer priorities.

By systematically developing a win strategy that integrates deep customer insights, competitive intelligence, and strategic alignment of capabilities, companies can significantly enhance their chances of not just winning an individual government contract but also establishing long-term relationships with clients. This strategic foresight into planning and execution makes your proposal not just a bid for a contract, but a comprehensive solution that addresses the client's needs both today and in the future.

7. Proposal Preparation: The insights and strategies developed during the capture phase facilitate an effective proposal development process once the RFP is released. Structured proposal methodologies, such as the Shipley method, are employed to ensure the proposal is compelling, compliant, and clearly articulates the value proposition.

The proposal preparation phase is critical to converting the insights and strategies from the capture phase into a winning bid. This phase demands meticulous attention to detail, adherence to RFP requirements, and strategic articulation of value propositions. Here's a detailed breakdown of the steps, skills, and personnel involved in building compliant, compelling, and effective proposals that are poised for success.

A. **Understanding and Compliance with RFP Requirements:**

The first step in proposal preparation is a thorough analysis of the Request for Proposal (RFP). This involves dissecting each requirement to ensure a full understanding of what the client expects. Compliance is key; every requirement must be addressed clearly in the proposal to avoid disqualification.

Skills Required:

- Attention to detail
- Analytical skills
- Legal and technical understanding

Personnel Involved:

- Proposal Manager
- Legal Advisor
- Subject Matter Experts (SMEs)

B. **Structuring the Proposal:**

Employ structured methodologies like the Shipley method to organize the proposal. This method guides the proposal team through each section of the proposal, ensuring that all critical elements are included:

- Executive Summary
- Technical Approach
- Management Plan
- Past Performance
- Cost Volume

Skills Required:

- Organizational skills
- Strategic thinking
- Writing and editing skills

Personnel Involved:

- Proposal Manager
- Technical Writers

- Editors

C. **Developing the Content:**

With the structure in place, the next step is to develop content that is not only compliant but also compelling. This involves translating the capture strategies and solutions into clear, concise, and persuasive text.

- **Technical Approach:** Describe how your proposed solution meets or exceeds the RFP requirements.
- **Management Plan:** Outline how the project will be managed to meet the client's goals.
- **Past Performance:** Demonstrate credibility with relevant examples of past successes.

Skills Required:

- Technical writing
- Project management
- Persuasive communication

Personnel Involved:

- Technical Writers
- Project Managers
- SMEs

D. **Reviewing and Refining the Proposal:**

Engage in multiple rounds of reviews to refine the proposal:

- **Pink Team Review:** Focuses on assessing the draft's alignment with the win strategy and RFP requirements.

- **Red Team Review:** A critical evaluation that simulates an external review, aimed at improving content quality and effectiveness.

Skills Required:

- Critical analysis
- Constructive feedback
- Detail-oriented review

Personnel Involved:

- Review Teams (Pink and Red Teams)
- Independent Reviewers
- Proposal Manager

E. **Finalizing and Submitting the Proposal:**

After incorporating all necessary revisions from the reviews, finalize the document. Ensure that the proposal is professionally formatted, free from errors, and compliant with submission guidelines.

- **Quality Control:** Conduct a final quality check to ensure there are no errors.
- **Submission:** Prepare the proposal for submission, adhering to the client's format and delivery requirements.

Skills Required:

- Quality control
- Attention to detail
- Time management

Personnel Involved:

- Quality Assurance Specialist
- Proposal Manager
- Administrative Support

F. **Post-Submission Follow-Up:**

After submission, prepare for potential follow-up queries from the client and post-submission presentations or demonstrations.

Skills Required:

- Communication
- Presentation skills
- Responsiveness

Personnel Involved:

- Business Development Team
- Technical Experts
- Proposal Manager

2020
SMALL BUSINESS CONFER
February 11-13, 2020 New Orleans, L
NATIONAL 8
ASSOCIATION

CHAPTER 4
PRACTICAL APPLICATION FOR SMALL BUSINESSES

Starting a small business in the government contracting sector can seem daunting, especially when resources are limited, and you might not have all the specialized positions filled. However, there are practical strategies that can help bridge the gap between your current capabilities and the demands of proposal development and contract management. Here's how you can maximize your existing resources while gradually building your company's capacity.

1. **Leverage Key Personnel**

You may not have a large team, but you can make the most of the talent you do have. Identify the key personnel within your organization who have multiple skills and can wear different hats. For instance, your business development manager might also have a strong grasp of project management or technical writing. Utilizing the diverse skills of your team members allows you to cover more ground without the immediate need for more hires.

In any business, but particularly in government contracting, leveraging key personnel effectively is the difference between operational efficiency and stagnation. Key personnel—whether they are executives, managers, or subject matter experts—carry the responsibility of driving strategic initiatives, executing the business plan, and ensuring the company remains competitive. However, for many small businesses, the reality is that key personnel may be limited to just one or two people, often including the founder. While large organizations have dedicated teams for business development, proposal writing, contract execution, and compliance, emerging businesses must maximize the skills and time of the few individuals they have.

The key to leveraging personnel effectively is time management, strategic delegation, and skill diversification. As the founder, you may be required to act as the CEO, business development officer, capture manager, and proposal writer all at once. This is not a disadvantage—it is an opportunity to develop an intimate knowledge of the contracting process and business functions. Rather than seeing limited personnel as a weakness, successful entrepreneurs view it as an advantage, allowing them to build a strong foundation before expanding the team.

Maximizing time is one of the most critical aspects of leveraging key personnel. Time is the most valuable asset in business, and when resources are scarce, time must be allocated with surgical precision. This requires setting clear priorities, automating repetitive tasks, and structuring the workday around high-value activities. For example, a founder who must handle both business development and proposal writing should allocate time strategically—focusing on networking and opportunity identification in the mornings, followed by proposal writing and administrative work in the afternoons. Breaking work into focused time blocks increases efficiency while ensuring that no critical task is overlooked.

Strategic delegation is another powerful method for leveraging key personnel. Even if there is only a small internal team, outsourcing or leveraging strategic partnerships can help distribute the workload effectively. For example, while the founder might handle proposal strategy and executive oversight, contracted writers, industry consultants, or virtual assistants can be brought in to assist with content development, compliance checks, or research. This allows the organization to function as a larger operation while keeping fixed costs low.

Additionally, encouraging cross-functional skills within the organization enables key personnel to handle multiple roles without sacrificing performance. For example, if an individual is skilled in business development, they should also be trained in proposal management and contract negotiation. This approach ensures that there is redundancy in skillsets, so the business does not become overly reliant on any one person for critical tasks. Continuous learning and professional development are essential for key personnel, ensuring they can adapt to the evolving demands of the contracting space.

Another essential factor is influence—getting key personnel to embrace the mindset of maximizing their own time and efficiency. This is where leadership and culture-building become crucial. Key personnel must understand the importance of their roles and the direct impact their contributions have on the company's success. A founder or executive who leads by example, demonstrating dedication, discipline, and strategic thinking, will naturally inspire the rest of the team to operate with the same level of commitment. Clear communication of goals and expectations ensures that everyone remains aligned with the company's mission.

Moreover, building external relationships and leveraging mentors, strategic partners, and industry contacts effectively extends the impact of key personnel. A well-connected founder can compensate for a small internal team by forming alliances with other industry professionals who can provide insights, referrals, or temporary support when needed. By leveraging relationships, small businesses can access resources, knowledge, and expertise that would otherwise require a much larger team to develop in-house.

Ultimately, leveraging key personnel is about working smarter, not harder. A small, highly efficient team with a clear strategic focus will always outperform a large, unstructured workforce. The key lies in prioritizing time effectively, fostering a culture of continuous learning, strategically delegating responsibilities, and developing strong industry relationships. The size of the team is not what determines success in government contracting; rather, it is the ability of the key personnel—whether that's one person or a small group—to make informed, strategic decisions and execute them with precision.

By embracing a proactive approach to personal and professional development, key personnel can evolve into multi-faceted leaders capable of handling diverse responsibilities. This adaptability is particularly crucial in government contracting, where opportunities are won by those who demonstrate expertise, credibility, and a deep understanding of customer needs. The ability to pivot between roles seamlessly—from strategy development to proposal writing to client engagement—gives small businesses an edge over larger firms that may be less agile.

To maintain long-term effectiveness, key personnel should consistently refine their skills. This means actively participating in industry conferences, attending government procurement training sessions, and becoming well-versed in regulations such as the Federal Acquisition Regulation (FAR) and the Defense Federal Acquisition Regulation Supplement (DFARS). These efforts ensure that key personnel are not only reactive to government requirements but positioned as experts who anticipate industry shifts and emerging opportunities.

Beyond skill enhancement, the ability to leverage technology significantly boosts productivity. Automation tools such as Customer Relationship Management (CRM) software, proposal management platforms, and artificial intelligence-driven data analysis tools allow small teams to function at the same level as larger competitors. Utilizing GovWin, SAM.gov alerts, and predictive analytics software can help key personnel track upcoming solicitations, assess competitor activity, and position the business for new contract opportunities.

Additionally, developing a standardized workflow ensures that key personnel remain focused on high-impact activities rather than getting lost in administrative tasks. Creating a repeatable process for capture management, proposal development, and contract administration eliminates inefficiencies and allows the team to scale operations without exponentially increasing workload. This structured approach ensures that every proposal is reviewed for compliance, competitive positioning, and strategic alignment before submission.

Networking and relationship-building remain integral aspects of leveraging key personnel. Success in government contracting often depends on who you know as much as what you know. Attending Small Business Administration (SBA) events, industry networking sessions, and matchmaking conferences enables key personnel to establish direct connections with contracting officers, prime contractors, and potential partners. These relationships not only provide insight into upcoming opportunities but also create pathways for subcontracting, mentor-protégé programs, and joint ventures.

To further optimize their influence, key personnel must master the art of thought leadership and branding. By publishing industry insights, engaging in panel discussions, and offering expertise in niche areas, key personnel enhance the company's reputation as a trusted authority in government contracting. This strategic positioning ensures that when decision-makers are considering vendors, they recognize the company's expertise and credibility, increasing the probability of contract awards.

Finally, self-discipline and resilience are essential qualities that key personnel must embody. The contracting process can be unpredictable, with long sales cycles, complex compliance requirements, and competitive pressures. Key personnel must cultivate a mindset of persistence, adaptability, and strategic problem-solving. Rather than viewing setbacks as failures, they should see them as opportunities to refine their approach, strengthen their capabilities, and position themselves for the next big win.

In conclusion, leveraging key personnel effectively—especially in the early stages of a company's growth—requires a combination of time management, strategic delegation, continuous learning, technology utilization, relationship-building, and personal branding. Whether it is one person wearing multiple hats or a small, agile team executing a focused strategy, the key to success lies in maximizing every resource, optimizing every decision, and positioning the business as a formidable competitor in the government contracting space.

2. **Focus on Strategic Outsourcing**

When certain expertise is required that is not available in-house, consider outsourcing as a cost-effective solution. Freelancers and consultants can fill critical gaps, such as proposal writing, graphic design, or specialized technical expertise. Platforms like Upwork, Freelancer, or specialized consulting firms offer access to professionals who can work on a project basis, providing the skills you need without the long-term financial commitment of full-time staff.

For small businesses, outsourcing is not merely a cost-cutting measure —it is a strategic necessity that enables entrepreneurs to operate efficiently, maximize resources, and focus on high-value activities. In the early stages of a business, particularly in government contracting, time, manpower, and expertise are limited commodities. The ability to delegate non-core tasks to specialized professionals can mean the difference between scaling efficiently and becoming overwhelmed by administrative burdens.

At its core, outsourcing allows businesses to access expertise without the long-term commitment of hiring full-time employees. Many small businesses operate with lean teams, where a single individual may be responsible for multiple functions such as business development, proposal writing, compliance management, and contract execution. While multitasking is a necessity in the early days, spreading key personnel too thin can result in missed opportunities, burnout, and decreased efficiency. Outsourcing provides a solution by allowing business owners to focus on strategic growth while specialists handle essential but time-consuming tasks.

One of the most immediate benefits of outsourcing is the ability to compete with larger firms by tapping into a global talent pool. A small government contracting firm, for example, may lack the internal expertise to write complex technical proposals, conduct compliance audits, or manage IT security requirements. However, by outsourcing these functions to freelancers, consultants, or external firms, the business can deliver high-quality work that meets federal requirements without carrying the overhead costs of a large team.

As a business grows, outsourcing becomes even more valuable, particularly in areas that require scalability. Administrative tasks such as payroll, accounting, contract management, and human resources can quickly become overwhelming as the company secures more contracts. Instead of diverting attention from business development to handle these responsibilities, many growing companies outsource administrative functions to professional firms, ensuring accuracy, efficiency, and compliance. This is especially important in government contracting, where financial mismanagement, improper invoicing, or regulatory non-compliance can result in penalties or contract termination.

Additionally, outsourcing allows businesses to adapt to fluctuating workloads without the risk of over-hiring or underutilizing employees. Government contracts often come with variable workloads—one quarter may involve intense proposal development, while the next may focus on project execution. Hiring full-time staff for every function may not be financially sustainable. By outsourcing proposal development, graphic design, IT support, or even legal services on an as-needed basis, businesses can scale their workforce dynamically, ensuring that resources are allocated efficiently.

Another crucial advantage of outsourcing is access to industry expertise and innovation. Many small businesses struggle to keep up with the latest federal regulations, procurement trends, and technological advancements. By outsourcing to subject matter experts, businesses gain insights that would otherwise take years to develop in-house. For example, contracting a government compliance consultant ensures that the business remains up to date with Federal Acquisition Regulation (FAR) and Defense Federal Acquisition Regulation Supplement (DFARS) changes, reducing legal risks and improving bid competitiveness. Similarly, outsourcing IT security and data management to cybersecurity firms ensures that sensitive contract data is protected without requiring the business to build an in-house IT department.

Outsourcing is also a powerful tool for enhancing business development and marketing efforts. Many small business owners are skilled in their technical field but lack the expertise to build brand awareness, generate leads, and craft persuasive marketing materials. By outsourcing content creation, website management, social media marketing, and proposal writing, businesses can establish a strong presence in their industry while focusing on their core competencies.

Perhaps most importantly, outsourcing enables business leaders to focus on high-value strategic decisions. Instead of getting bogged down in administrative tasks, technical writing, or compliance documentation, owners and executives can dedicate their time to building relationships with contracting officers, identifying new opportunities, negotiating partnerships, and positioning the business for long-term success. This ability to remain strategically focused while leveraging external expertise is a hallmark of successful government contractors.

As businesses continue to grow, outsourcing transitions from a tactical solution to a long-term business strategy. Large firms often outsource entire divisions such as customer support, supply chain management, or IT infrastructure, allowing them to remain agile and cost-effective while maintaining a focus on core operations. What begins as a means of survival for a small business evolves into a competitive advantage, enabling companies to scale efficiently, maintain flexibility, and achieve sustained growth in the marketplace.

Ultimately, outsourcing is not about reducing responsibility—it is about optimizing it. Knowing when to outsource tasks, whom to outsource to, and how to integrate external support effectively ensures that businesses can operate efficiently, remain competitive, and grow without being constrained by internal limitations. Whether a business is just starting out or expanding into new markets, strategic outsourcing remains one of the most powerful tools for maximizing productivity, increasing profitability, and ensuring long-term sustainability in government contracting and beyond.

Strategic Teaming with Larger Firms: Balancing Revenue and Competitive Strength in Government Contracting

Teaming with larger firms is often a necessary and strategic move for small businesses looking to compete effectively in the federal contracting arena. While small businesses can leverage agility, cost efficiency, and set-aside advantages, larger firms bring established past performance, specialized capabilities, and existing relationships with government agencies. However, one of the realities of teaming with a larger firm is the potential need to sacrifice a greater percentage of the contract's revenue in exchange for their expertise and resources. While this can seem like a significant trade-off, the strategic advantages gained through such partnerships can ultimately position the small business for long-term success and increased competitiveness.

One of the primary reasons small businesses team with larger firms is to bridge capability gaps that might otherwise prevent them from competing for or winning a contract. In federal procurement, agencies evaluate not just price but also technical competency, management capability, and the contractor's ability to mitigate risks and meet performance requirements. A small business that lacks experience with large-scale government programs, specialized technologies, or security clearances may find itself at a disadvantage when bidding against more established competitors. By teaming with a larger firm that possesses these capabilities, the small business can enhance its proposal, making it more attractive to the government evaluation team.

However, securing a teaming agreement often requires the smaller prime contractor to allocate a significant percentage of the contract's work—and consequently, the revenue—to the larger partner. This is particularly true for contracts that involve highly technical services, where the larger firm may hold key certifications, proprietary technology, or specialized personnel that the small business lacks. While this revenue split can reduce the immediate financial gain for the small business, the strategic benefit is that it makes the overall bid stronger, improving the likelihood of winning the contract over a larger prime competitor.

One of the most valuable aspects of teaming with a larger firm is the opportunity to improve the Past Performance Evaluation (PPE) score, a critical factor in future government contracting opportunities. The federal government places significant emphasis on past performance when awarding contracts, and small businesses that lack experience managing large contracts can struggle to compete against firms with extensive track records. By teaming with a well-established firm, the small business gains access to contract experience that it can later leverage in future proposals, enabling it to compete for more lucrative prime contracts without needing a larger partner in the future.

Additionally, teaming arrangements can help small businesses mitigate financial and operational risks. Government contracts often require upfront capital, extensive compliance measures, and strict regulatory adherence. Many small businesses struggle with the financial burden of managing payroll, securing insurance, meeting cybersecurity require-ments (such as CMMC compliance), and ensuring contract execution within federal guidelines. A larger teaming partner can shoulder some of these burdens, allowing the small business to focus on its core areas of expertise while reducing the financial strain of contract execution.

Another key advantage of teaming with larger firms is the ability to gain insights into how top-tier contractors operate within the federal procurement space. By collaborating with a more experienced partner, the small business can learn best practices for proposal writing, contract negotiations, compliance management, and performance execution. This knowledge is invaluable as the small business grows, enabling it to compete more effectively as a standalone prime contractor in future bids.

Moreover, teaming with a larger firm can improve the small business's standing when competing against other large firms. In government procurements that involve full and open competition, small businesses often face formidable competition from billion-dollar corporations that have vast resources and long-standing government relationships. However, by structuring a teaming agreement with a large firm that enhances the proposal's technical credibility, risk mitigation, and pricing competitiveness, the small business may actually outmaneuver larger prime competitors who are bidding alone. This is particularly true when the government seeks innovation, agility, and cost-effectiveness—qualities that small businesses are known for but that may be strengthened further through teaming arrangements.

While the decision to give up a larger percentage of revenue in a teaming agreement should be carefully weighed, it is important to recognize that the true value of teaming extends beyond immediate financial gain. The benefits include enhanced credibility, improved past performance records, reduced operational risk, and greater access to future contracting opportunities. In the long run, these advantages often outweigh the short-term revenue trade-off, especially if the small business strategically positions itself to leverage the experience gained through these partnerships to compete more independently in the future.

Ultimately, teaming with larger firms should be approached as an investment in growth and market positioning rather than just a financial transaction. The key to a successful partnership lies in structuring agreements that balance risk and reward, ensuring that both parties contribute value while aligning with the strategic goals of the small business. With the right approach, teaming with a larger firm not only increases the probability of winning government contracts but also sets the foundation for sustained success and expansion in the competitive federal marketplace.

3. **Use Technology and Tools**

Technology has become an indispensable asset in the world of government contracting, allowing businesses to conduct market research, track competitor activity, streamline proposal development, and manage contract execution more efficiently. Tools such as GovWin, PartsBase.com, and project management software have transformed the way companies gather intelligence, develop strategies, and position themselves for success. These platforms provide small and growing businesses with the same level of insight and operational efficiency as larger, more established competitors, ensuring they can remain competitive in a rapidly evolving market.

GovWin, operated by Deltek, is one of the most powerful competitive intelligence and market research tools available to government contractors. It allows businesses to track upcoming opportunities, analyze agency spending trends, and gain insights into competitors' federal contract activity. By leveraging GovWin, businesses can identify potential opportunities before they are formally announced, giving them a head start in the capture management process. This early visibility allows contractors to build relationships with government buyers, position their offerings strategically, and align their proposals with the agency's objectives long before a Request for Proposal (RFP) is released. Additionally, GovWin's extensive database of past contracts and award data provides invaluable intelligence on pricing trends, winning strategies, and subcontracting opportunities, enabling businesses to refine their approach and increase their probability of winning (P-Win) scores.

For companies working with defense and aerospace components, PartsBase.com serves as a crucial tool for researching parts availability, pricing, and suppliers. This platform allows contractors to search for specific parts required for military and defense contracts, identify approved vendors, and obtain pricing benchmarks. By utilizing PartsBase, businesses can improve their supply chain efficiency, ensure compliance with sourcing regulations, and develop cost-competitive pricing strategies. The ability to quickly identify alternative suppliers, evaluate lead times, and verify part authenticity can make the differnce between delivering on time and losing a contract due to supply chain inefficiencies.

Beyond competitive research and procurement intelligence, technology also plays a vital role in proposal management and collaboration. Government contracting requires a highly structured and disciplined approach to proposal writing, often involving multiple contributors working on various sections of a bid simultaneously. Platforms such as Microsoft Teams, Google Workspace, and SharePoint enable teams to collaborate in real-time, ensuring seamless document sharing, version control, and communication across dispersed teams. These tools allow businesses to streamline the proposal development process by assigning tasks, setting deadlines, and ensuring compliance with formatting and submission requirements.

Project management platforms such as Trello, Asana, and Monday.com help businesses organize their workflow, track progress, and maintain visibility over every stage of the capture and proposal development process. By using these tools, small teams can break down complex proposal tasks into manageable steps, set milestones, and ensure accountability among team members. These platforms also provide automated reminders and notifications, ensuring that critical deadlines are met and that proposals remain on schedule.

In addition to collaborative and project management tools, businesses must also leverage data analytics and automation platforms to optimize their government contracting strategies. Tools such as Bloomberg Government (BGov), SAM.gov alerts, and FPDS (Federal Procurement Data System) allow companies to track agency procurement trends, identify key decision-makers, and assess historical contract performance data. These platforms provide critical insights into which agencies are spending money, what types of contracts are being awarded, and which companies are consistently winning bids. Armed with this information, businesses can tailor their proposals to align with agency priorities, differentiate themselves from competitors, and improve thei chances of securing contracts.

Cybersecurity and compliance are also critical considerations fo government contractors. With the increasing emphasis on CMMC (Cybersecurity Maturity Model Certification) compliance for defens contracts, businesses must adopt secure document storage, encryptec communication channels, and risk assessment tools to protect sensitiv government data. Platforms such as Box for Government, AWS GovCloud, and Microsoft Azure Government provide secure cloud based solutions that meet federal compliance standards, ensuring tha contractors remain eligible for opportunities requiring strict data secu rity protocols.

Finally, automation tools such as AI-driven proposal generators pricing optimization software, and customer relationship managemen (CRM) systems have become game-changers for small businesse looking to scale their government contracting operations. CRM tool like Salesforce, HubSpot, and Zoho CRM allow businesses to trac client interactions, manage agency relationships, and automate follow ups, ensuring that they remain engaged with key government buyer and procurement officers. AI-driven proposal generators, such a Proposify and Loopio, assist businesses in quickly generating proposa templates, ensuring compliance, and improving content consistency reducing the time and effort required for each submission.

By integrating these technologies into their daily operations, small busi nesses can level the playing field against larger competitors, improv efficiency, and enhance their ability to win government contracts. Th combination of competitive intelligence platforms, collaborativ proposal tools, automation software, and cybersecurity measure enables businesses to execute high-quality bids, maintain compliance and develop strategic partnerships with government agencies. A federal procurement continues to evolve, leveraging the right tech nology stack will remain a critical factor in sustaining growth, main taining a competitive edge, and successfully navigating the complexities of the government contracting industry.

here are numerous affordable or even free tools that can help streamline the proposal development process and improve collaboration among your team. Project management software like Trello, Asana, or Monday.com can help keep your proposal development tasks on track. For document collaboration, Google Workspace or Microsoft Teams can be invaluable, allowing multiple team members to work on documents simultaneously and communicate effectively.

The Role of Artificial Intelligence in Government Contracting: Leveraging AI-Driven Tools for Competitive Advantage

Artificial intelligence (AI) has revolutionized the way businesses approach government contracting, market research, proposal development, and relationship management. AI-powered platforms streamline the capture process, automate data collection, optimize pricing models, and enhance competitive intelligence, allowing small businesses to operate with the efficiency and precision of larger enterprises. Leveraging AI-driven tools such as Seamless.AI, ChatGPT for proposal writing, Predictive Analytics for pricing optimization, and AI-driven CRM systems enables companies to make data-driven decisions, refine their strategy, and increase their probability of winning (P-Win) scores.

One of the most powerful AI-driven tools available to government contractors is Seamless.AI, a real-time search and contact intelligence platform that helps businesses identify and connect with key decision-makers in federal procurement. This tool automates the process of finding contracting officers, program managers, and agency buyers, providing up-to-date contact information, organizational structures, and outreach strategies. In government contracting, where relationships play a crucial role, Seamless.AI helps businesses bypass gatekeepers and directly engage with the individuals responsible for awarding contracts. By automating lead generation and outreach, small businesses can significantly enhance their networking and relationship-building efforts, ensuring they remain top-of-mind when opportunities arise.

AI-powered tools such as Bid Intelligence Platforms (Bloomberg Government, AI-driven GovWin Extensions, and GovTribe) use machine learning algorithms to analyze procurement trends, predict upcoming RFPs, and identify which agencies are actively spending on specific NAICS codes. Instead of manually sifting through Federal Procurement Data System (FPDS) reports or daily SAM.gov updates, businesses can use AI to filter relevant opportunities, assess market demand, and receive tailored recommendations for bids that align with their capabilities. These AI-driven insights ensure that businesses do not waste time chasing low-probability contracts and instead focus their resources on high-probability, high-value opportunities.

AI also plays a pivotal role in proposal automation and optimization. Tools such as ChatGPT, Grammarly, and Proposify allow businesses to generate, refine, and proofread complex government proposals in a fraction of the time it would take manually. AI-driven proposal generators can auto-fill compliance sections, integrate past performance references, and recommend improvements based on previous successful bids. By leveraging AI for technical writing, formatting, and compliance reviews, businesses reduce human error, enhance proposal clarity, and ensure their submissions align with government evaluation criteria.

For pricing strategies, AI-driven platforms such as Price-to-Win (PTW) Analytics, Costpoint by Deltek, and PriceEdge AI allow contractors to benchmark their pricing against industry standards, analyze competitor pricing models, and optimize their cost structures to remain both competitive and profitable. In government contracting, overpricing can eliminate a bid from consideration, while underpricing can lead to unsustainable project execution. AI-driven pricing tools help businesses strike the perfect balance, ensuring they remain cost-competitive while maintaining profitability.

AI-powered Customer Relationship Management (CRM) systems such as Salesforce Einstein, Zoho AI, and HubSpot AI further streamline business development by automating follow-ups, tracking email engagement, and predicting which contracting officers are most likely to issue future solicitations. By analyzing past interactions, contract award patterns, and procurement behaviors, these tools help businesses prioritize outreach efforts and engage with agencies at the right time.

AI-driven chatbots and virtual assistants are also transforming how businesses interact with government buyers and subcontracting partners. Platforms such as Drift AI and Chatfuel allow companies to automate initial inquiries, schedule meetings, and answer frequently asked questions about capabilities and contract availability. This ensures that potential buyers receive instant responses, improving engagement rates and increasing the likelihood of securing government contracts.

Beyond proposal development and outreach, AI is enhancing supply chain and logistics management, a critical factor in government contracting, particularly in defense and manufacturing. AI-powered supply chain platforms such as Llamasoft AI, Resilinc, and SAP Leonardo use machine learning to predict supplier disruptions, optimize procurement strategies, and ensure contractors meet federal delivery requirements. These tools provide real-time insights into inventory levels, risk assessments, and sourcing alternatives, ensuring that businesses remain compliant with government regulations such as the Berry Amendment and Buy American Act.

Cybersecurity and compliance automation are also benefiting from AI advancements. With increasing government regulations such as CMMC (Cybersecurity Maturity Model Certification) and NIST 800-171, AI-powered compliance tools such as Darktrace AI, IBM Watson Security, and Microsoft Defender AI help businesses automate threat detection, monitor network vulnerabilities, and generate compliance reports for contract audits. By leveraging AI for cybersecurity compliance, businesses reduce the risk of data breaches, contract violations, and costly penalties.

AI-driven predictive analytics platforms such as Palantir Government AI, Tableau AI, and SAS Analytics allow businesses to forecast contract win rates, analyze industry shifts, and make data-driven business decisions. These tools process millions of data points from federal procurement databases, economic reports, and competitor activities, providing businesses with actionable insights on when, where, and how to bid most effectively.

The integration of AI into government contracting is not just a competitive advantage—it is becoming a necessity for survival in an increasingly digital procurement landscape. Companies that effectively leverage AI-driven tools can automate time-consuming tasks, improve efficiency, enhance compliance, and significantly increase their probability of winning federal contracts. As AI technology continues to evolve, businesses that stay ahead of the curve by adopting intelligent automation, machine learning, and data analytics will be best positioned for long-term success in the highly competitive world of government procurement.

4. **Develop In-House Training**

As you grow, invest in training your current staff to develop the skills needed for future proposals. Online courses, webinars, and workshops —many of which are specifically designed for government contracting —can be cost-effective ways to build your team's capabilities. This not only enhances your team's skills but also boosts morale by showing your commitment to their professional development.

Developing in-house training is a strategic investment that not only strengthens a company's workforce but also enhances its ability to compete for and execute government contracts effectively. As a company grows, the need for a well-trained, knowledgeable team becomes increasingly important. Government contracting requires specialized skills in compliance, proposal development, pricing strategies, contract administration, and project execution. Without ongoing training, employees may struggle to navigate the complexities of federal acquisition regulations, proposal writing requirements, and contract management standards. Establishing an in-house training program allows businesses to tailor their workforce development efforts to align with both immediate project needs and long-term strategic goals.

Creating a structured in-house training program begins with assessing the company's specific needs. It is essential to evaluate existing skill gaps and identify areas where employees need additional expertise. This process includes reviewing past contract performance, analyzing proposal win rates, and assessing feedback from contracting officers to determine areas for improvement. Once the knowledge gaps are identified, a structured curriculum should be designed to address the most critical areas of government contracting. Training modules should include essential topics such as compliance with Federal Acquisition Regulation (FAR) and Defense Federal Acquisition Regulation Supplement (DFARS), cost estimating and price-to-win strategies, proposal writing techniques, government contract negotiation, and subcontractor management.

Effective in-house training should incorporate multiple learning methods to accommodate different employee learning styles. Online courses, instructor-led workshops, mentorship programs, and hands-on exercises all contribute to a well-rounded training experience. Webinars, recorded training sessions, and interactive e-learning platforms provide employees with flexible, self-paced learning opportunities, while live training sessions encourage direct engagement and immediate feedback. Case studies and real-world examples should be integrated into the curriculum to reinforce practical applications of government contracting principles. Bringing in external experts or guest speakers who have extensive experience in federal procurement can provide additional insights and reinforce best practices.

For companies that may not have the internal expertise to develop a comprehensive training program, Nijsha Enterprise, Inc. is ready and willing to provide consulting services to assist with in-house training development. Nijsha Enterprise understands the challenges that small businesses face in acquiring the necessary knowledge and skills to compete in the federal contracting space. Through customized consulting services, Nijsha Enterprise helps businesses design training programs that are specifically tailored to their industry, contract focus areas, and workforce development goals. Whether a company is looking to enhance its proposal writing skills, improve its contract compliance capabilities, or develop a strategic pricing approach, Nijsha Enterprise provides the guidance needed to build a high-performing team.

One of the most critical aspects of in-house training is ensuring that the knowledge gained is applied in real-time. Employees should have opportunities to practice their newly acquired skills through mock proposal exercises, contract simulations, and bid strategy workshops. This hands-on approach reinforces learning and allows employees to gain confidence in applying best practices. To track progress, companies should establish key performance indicators (KPIs) to measure training effectiveness. Metrics such as improved proposal quality, increased bid success rates, enhanced compliance adherence, and employee competency evaluations provide tangible evidence of training impact.

Beyond technical skills, in-house training also plays a crucial role in fostering a culture of continuous learning and professional growth. Employees who feel that their company invests in their development are more likely to be engaged, motivated, and committed to long-term success. By implementing structured training initiatives, businesses not only build a more knowledgeable workforce but also create an environment that values expertise and continuous improvement.

As businesses expand their government contracting efforts, the ability to train and retain skilled personnel becomes a competitive advantage. Investing in employee development reduces the dependency on external consultants, improves operational efficiency, and ensures that the company remains compliant with evolving government regulations. Nijsha Enterprise, Inc. recognizes that a company's greatest asset is its people, and by equipping employees with the right skills, businesses can position themselves for sustainable growth in the government contracting industry.

For companies that are unsure of where to start, Nijsha Enterprise offers tailored consultation services to develop in-house training programs that align with specific contracting goals. Through workshops, curriculum development, training materials, and mentorship, Nijsha Enterprise ensures that businesses have the tools and knowledge needed to compete and succeed in the federal market. Whether a business is new to government contracting or looking to enhance its existing capabilities, an effective training program is a foundational element for long-term success.

5. Build Relationships for Team Augmentation

Networking is crucial in the government contracting world. Building relationships with other small businesses can lead to partnerships where you can share resources or collaborate on contracts. Joining industry groups, attending conferences, and participating in local business events can connect you with potential partners who complement your capabilities.

Attending industry trade shows, seminars, symposiums, and networking events is one of the most valuable ways to build and maintain relationships in the government contracting space. These gatherings provide opportunities to engage directly with government procurement officers, prime contractors, subcontractors, and industry experts, creating a pathway to long-term business relationships that can lead to contract awards and strategic partnerships. The government contracting landscape is highly competitive, and success often depends not only on a company's technical capabilities but also on its ability to develop strong relationships with key stakeholders. Trade shows and industry events offer the perfect environment to showcase a company's expertise, learn about upcoming opportunities, and forge connections that can evolve into teaming agreements or subcontracting opportunities.

One of the greatest advantages of attending these events is the ability to meet decision-makers face-to-face. Government contracting involves layers of bureaucracy, and in many cases, securing a contract starts with being known and trusted within the industry. By attending trade shows and engaging with contracting officers and industry leaders, businesses can gain firsthand insights into what government agencies are looking for and how to tailor their proposals to meet those expectations. Additionally, networking at these events helps companies stay ahead of market trends, understand policy changes, and identify upcoming contracting opportunities that may not yet be publicly advertised.

Specific trade shows and symposiums cater to different sectors within government contracting, making it essential for businesses to target the right events. For companies involved in defense and aerospace contracting, events such as the Association of the United States Army (AUSA) Annual Meeting & Exposition, the Air Force Association (AFA) Air, Space & Cyber Conference, and the Navy League's Sea-Air-Space Exposition provide unparalleled access to key decision-makers in the Department of Defense and major defense contractors. These events allow businesses to engage directly with military procurement officers, defense primes, and technology innovators, opening doors to new opportunities in military contracts.

For companies focused on cybersecurity, artificial intelligence, and IT services, events such as the RSA Conference, AFCEA WEST, and the National Cyber Summit provide insight into government priorities and emerging technologies that impact procurement decisions. Cybersecurity is a growing concern for government agencies, and these events offer contractors an opportunity to align their offerings with federal security initiatives, such as CMMC (Cybersecurity Maturity Model Certification) compliance and zero-trust architectures.

Businesses working in general government contracting and infrastructure projects benefit from attending events such as the Government Procurement Conference (GPC), the National Contract Management Association (NCMA) World Congress, and the Small Business Administration's (SBA) National Small Business Week Conference. These gatherings focus on procurement best practices, small business engagement, and federal contracting opportunities across various industries, including construction, logistics, healthcare, and professional services.

Trade shows and symposiums also provide an excellent platform for networking with potential teaming partners. Large prime contractors often attend these events to find small businesses to fulfill subcontracting requirements for government contracts. By establishing relationships with these primes, small businesses can position themselves for subcontracting opportunities that serve as a stepping stone toward securing larger prime contracts. Moreover, engaging with industry associations such as the National Defense Industrial Association (NDIA), the Professional Services Council (PSC), and the Armed Forces Communications and Electronics Association (AFCEA) helps businesses integrate into well-established networks that facilitate teaming arrangements and mentor-protégé programs.

Another critical advantage of attending industry events is the opportunity to stay informed about government policies, acquisition strategies, and budget priorities. Many conferences include keynote speeches from high-ranking government officials, panel discussions with procurement leaders, and workshops that dive deep into regulatory changes affecting federal contracting. Understanding the direction of government spending and agency priorities allows businesses to align their strategies and prepare for upcoming procurement opportunities.

The relationships built at these events are not static; they require ongoing engagement and renewal. Government contracting is an ever-evolving landscape where agency needs change, personnel turnover occurs, and new initiatives emerge. By continuously attending industry events, businesses maintain relevance, reinforce existing relationships, and develop new connections that can translate into future contract opportunities. Networking is not a one-time activity but a continuous process that ensures long-term success.

Ultimately, industry trade shows, seminars, and networking events serve as the foundation for building relationships that drive business growth in government contracting. They provide a direct pathway to integration with key players in the industry, ensuring that businesses remain visible, informed, and competitive. Companies that actively participate in these events position themselves for greater success by increasing their credibility, expanding their network, and staying ahead of market trends. Whether through direct engagement with contracting officers, teaming with prime contractors, or gaining insights into industry developments, attending these events is an essential strategy for any business looking to thrive in the government marketplace.

6. **Start Small and Scale Gradually**

Begin by targeting smaller contracts or subcontracts that are manageable with your current resources. This approach allows you to build a track record and gain valuable experience without being overwhelmed. As you successfully complete projects and your revenue grows, you can reinvest in expanding your team and capabilities.

Controlled and Sustained Growth: Scaling a Business for Long-Term Success in Government Contracting

Scaling a business in government contracting requires a deliberate, strategic approach to ensure that growth is sustainable and aligned with market demand, financial stability, and regulatory requirements. Controlled and sustained growth allows a company to maintain operational efficiency, meet contract obligations without overextending resources, and establish a reputation for reliability in the government marketplace. Many businesses in federal contracting fail not because they lack opportunities, but because they expand too quickly, taking on contracts beyond their financial and operational capacity. Proper scaling requires sound financial management, regulatory compliance, and a clear understanding of how banks, investors, and government agencies evaluate a company's growth trajectory.

The Role of Financial Institutions and Investors in Business Growth

Banks and investors closely monitor key financial indicators to determine a company's ability to scale while maintaining financial health. Liquidity, revenue stability, debt-to-equity ratios, cash flow management, and historical performance on contracts are critical factors in determining whether a business can sustain growth. Government contractors must ensure that they have sufficient working capital to meet payroll, procure materials, and cover operational costs while awaiting government payments, which can sometimes take months due to federal invoicing cycles.

Lenders and investors also examine a company's past performance through the Federal Procurement Data System (FPDS) and the Contractor Performance Assessment Reporting System (CPARS) to evaluate whether a business has successfully executed contracts without performance deficiencies. A strong CPARS rating increases a company's credibility and attractiveness to investors who may consider financing expansion efforts through lines of credit, Small Business Administration (SBA) loans, or private equity funding. Many small businesses in government contracting rely on SBA 7(a) loans and SBA 504 loans to fund initial scaling efforts, allowing them to invest in infrastructure, hiring, and new business development initiatives.

Additionally, investors track whether a business is growing through diversification or over-concentration. A company that secures multiple contracts across different federal agencies, contract types, and NAICS codes is often seen as a safer investment than a business that is overly reliant on a single agency or contract vehicle. Diversification helps mitigate risk and ensures revenue stability even if budget shifts or policy changes reduce funding in one sector.

Government Oversight on Business Growth

The federal government actively tracks the growth of small businesses through annual revenue thresholds and employee count limits set by the SBA's NAICS size standards. The Code of Federal Regulations (CFR) 13 CFR 121.201 outlines size standards for each NAICS code, dictating whether a business qualifies as small. As a business grows, it must monitor whether its three-year average revenue or employee count surpasses the threshold for its designated industry.

Once a company exceeds its NAICS size standard, it is no longer eligible for set-aside contracts under small business programs such as the 8(a) Business Development Program, Women-Owned Small Business (WOSB) Program, HUBZone Program, and Service-Disabled Veteran-Owned Small Business (SDVOSB) Program. This transition, often referred to as graduating from small business status, presents both challenges and opportunities. A company must now compete head-to-head with large federal contractors, requiring adjustments in pricing strategies, teaming agreements, and contract capture approaches.

Businesses preparing to transition out of small business status must implement a large-business strategy before officially graduating. This includes securing long-term relationships with government agencies, developing strong subcontracting partnerships, obtaining certifications such as ISO 9001 or CMMI, and positioning themselves for full-and-open competition contracts. Many companies in this stage pursue joint ventures, mentor-protégé agreements, and strategic mergers to strengthen their competitive positioning in the large business space.

Regulatory Considerations for Growth and Scaling

As businesses expand, they must remain compliant with Federal Acquisition Regulation (FAR) and Defense Federal Acquisition Regulation Supplement (DFARS) clauses that govern financial stability, cybersecurity, and subcontracting requirements. The FAR 19.301-2 outlines how businesses must recertify their size status after mergers or acquisitions, while DFARS 252.242-7005 mandates that contractors maintain an adequate business system to manage increased financial and operational complexity.

For businesses scaling into the mid-tier market, FAR Part 42 on contract administration provides guidance on financial responsibility, performance tracking, and compliance with agency requirements. Additionally, companies that surpass small business size standards but are not yet considered large enterprises often seek graduated set-aside transition strategies, where they team with small businesses to remain competitive on contracts that include small business participation requirements.

Cybersecurity also becomes a growing concern as businesses scale, particularly in defense contracting. The CMMC (Cybersecurity Maturity Model Certification) framework, as outlined in DFARS 252.204-7012, mandates that companies handling Controlled Unclassified Information (CUI) implement stringent cybersecurity measures to qualify for future contracts. As a company expands, investing in cybersecurity infrastructure and compliance tools ensures continued eligibility for federal contracts.

Strategies for Controlled and Sustainable Growth

Sustained growth requires a balanced approach that integrates financial planning, operational capacity, regulatory compliance, and market positioning. Companies that attempt to scale too quickly without ensuring they have the necessary capital, personnel, and administrative systems in place risk contract failures that can damage their reputation and CPARS ratings. A deliberate approach to growth includes:

- Pacing expansion based on actual contract awards rather than speculative opportunities. Businesses should only bid on contracts they have the infrastructure to support, ensuring that delivery quality remains high.
- Developing a financial cushion to weather delays in contract funding and payments. Many government contractors face payment delays due to government invoicing cycles, and a lack of cash reserves can cripple expansion efforts.
- Investing in personnel training and leadership development. As a company grows, leadership must shift from day-to-day operations to strategic management, ensuring that new hires can handle execution while executives focus on business development.
- Positioning for full-and-open competition contracts before outgrowing small business status. Companies should gradually expand into unrestricted competitions, building a track record that will help them transition successfully into the large business market.

For companies anticipating outgrowing their small business designation, a common strategy is to merge with, be acquired by, or acquire another company to expand capabilities and enhance competitiveness.

Many businesses position themselves for acquisition by larger federal contractors seeking to add small business past performance and agency relationships to their portfolios. Others choose to merge with mid-tier contractors to create stronger joint ventures capable of winning full-and-open competitions.

Ultimately, controlled and sustained growth is about strategic decision-making, financial discipline, and long-term positioning. The federal government, investors, and industry stakeholders all evaluate a company's ability to scale based on its past performance, financial stability, and ability to comply with regulatory requirements. Businesses that grow too fast without the proper controls risk contract failures, loss of eligibility for set-aside programs, and financial distress. However, those that scale strategically, maintain compliance, and build the right relationships will successfully transition from small business status to becoming a formidable player in the federal contracting industry.

7. **Streamline Your Focus**

Concentrate on opportunities that align closely with your core competencies and where you can deliver the most value. This focused approach reduces the complexity of proposals and increases your chances of success. As your business grows and stabilizes, you can then consider expanding into new areas.

One of the most important strategies for small businesses entering the government contracting space is streamlining their focus to align with core competencies. Many companies make the mistake of chasing every available opportunity, believing that casting a wide net will increase their chances of winning contracts. However, this approach often leads to wasted resources, unfocused proposals, and ultimately, a lower probability of success. Instead, companies that strategically concentrate on opportunities that align closely with their expertise, past performance, and existing capabilities are far more likely to establish a strong foothold and build a reputation for excellence.

A well-defined focus allows a company to become known for a particular set of skills, services, or products within the federal marketplace. Government agencies look for contractors who can deliver highly specialized and reliable solutions rather than generalists who may lack depth in a particular area. By identifying and refining niche strengths, businesses can develop a competitive advantage, making it easier to win contracts in specific areas and build credibility within their targeted agencies. Whether a company specializes in cybersecurity, logistics, facility maintenance, or software development, concentrating on a core area ensures that resources are allocated effectively, capabilities are maximized, and the proposal process is streamlined.

The ability to streamline focus begins with conducting a thorough assessment of the company's strengths, unique value propositions, and areas of competitive advantage. This includes analyzing past performance, employee expertise, and existing relationships with government agencies. By identifying what the company does best and where it has the highest probability of success, leadership can make data-driven decisions about which opportunities to pursue and which to decline. Tools like GovWin, SAM.gov, and FPDS (Federal Procurement Data System) can help identify contract opportunities that align with these core strengths, ensuring that the company bids on contracts where it has a legitimate competitive edge.

Focusing on a specific market segment also simplifies the proposal development process. When companies bid on contracts that align with their core competencies, they already have much of the required documentation, certifications, and past performance references readily available. This reduces the time and effort needed to prepare compelling proposals, allowing businesses to respond to opportunities more efficiently and increase their win rates. Instead of crafting proposals from scratch for every solicitation, companies with a focused approach can leverage standardized proposal templates, pre-developed technical solutions, and case studies that demonstrate expertise in a specific field. This level of preparation results in higher-quality submissions and a stronger alignment with government evaluation criteria.

Another benefit of maintaining a focused strategy is the ability to build deep, long-term relationships with government agencies. Contracting officers, program managers, and procurement specialists prefer to work with vendors they trust and who have demonstrated consistent success in a particular area. By developing a reputation for excellence within a focused niche, businesses can establish themselves as go-to contractors for specific services or solutions. This not only increases the likelihood of contract renewals and extensions but also leads to invitations for sole-source contracts or limited competition procurements, further strengthening the company's position in the market.

As a business grows and stabilizes, expanding into new areas can be considered, but only when the company has the operational capacity, financial resources, and subject matter expertise to support diversification. Many successful government contractors start with a single NAICS code and gradually expand into adjacent markets once they have established a solid foundation. This type of strategic growth allows businesses to scale responsibly without overextending themselves or diluting their core competencies.

Additionally, streamlining focus does not mean ignoring new opportunities; rather, it means approaching growth strategically. Companies should continually monitor market trends, emerging government needs, and technological advancements to identify areas where their existing expertise can be leveraged in new ways. If an expansion opportunity arises that aligns closely with the company's strengths, leadership can explore partnerships, teaming arrangements, or mentor-protégé programs to gain a foothold in new areas without taking on excessive risk.

Ultimately, streamlining focus is about efficiency, strategic positioning, and long-term sustainability. Companies that remain disciplined in their approach, concentrate on contracts that align with their strengths, and build deep expertise in a specific area are far more likely to succeed in the competitive world of government contracting. This focused approach results in stronger proposals, higher win rates, and a more efficient allocation of resources. Over time, this strategy not only enhances a company's reputation but also creates a foundation for sustainable growth, allowing businesses to scale with confidence and expand their capabilities in a deliberate and measured way.

How Nijsha Enterprise, Inc. has become known as a leader

Nijsha Enterprise, Inc. has established itself as a premier provider of cabling, printed circuit boards, wire harness production, and reverse engineering services in both the federal government contracting business and the commercial contracting sector. Through years of strategic growth, technical excellence, and a relentless commitment to quality, Nijsha has built a reputation as a trusted partner for mission-critical projects requiring precision engineering and advanced manufacturing capabilities.

Cabling and wire harness production have been at the core of Nijsha Enterprise's operations, providing essential components for a wide range of applications in defense, aerospace, telecommunications, and industrial automation. The company's expertise in designing, assembling, and testing custom wire harnesses ensures seamless integration with complex electronic systems used in military aircraft, ground vehicles, and naval vessels. By adhering to the highest industry standards, including MIL-SPEC and IPC/WHMA-A-620 requirements, Nijsha delivers products that meet stringent government and commercial specifications. These capabilities have positioned the company as a key supplier for Department of Defense contracts, providing critical support to prime contractors and federal agencies that depend on high-reliability wiring solutions for national security applications.

Printed circuit board (PCB) manufacturing has also become a major area of specialization for Nijsha Enterprise, serving both government and commercial customers in need of high-performance electronic assemblies. As modern defense and commercial systems grow increasingly dependent on miniaturized, high-density electronics, Nijsha has remained at the forefront of PCB innovation. The company produces a wide range of circuit boards, from simple single-layer designs to highly complex multi-layer configurations with embedded components and high-speed signal processing capabilities. By investing in advanced manufacturing technologies and rigorous quality assurance protocols, Nijsha ensures that its PCBs meet the reliability and performance standards required for mission-critical applications.

Reverse engineering has been another area where Nijsha Enterprise has built a formidable reputation, helping both government and private-sector clients extend the life cycle of legacy equipment and replace obsolete components. Many military and aerospace systems rely on aging electronic assemblies that are no longer supported by their original manufacturers. Nijsha's expertise in reverse engineering enables it to analyze, replicate, and improve upon these components, ensuring continued functionality without the need for costly system-wide upgrades. This capability has been instrumental in supporting sustainment programs for the U.S. military, reducing costs while maintaining operational readiness for critical defense assets. The company's reverse engineering services also extend to commercial industries, providing cost-effective solutions for businesses looking to modernize aging equipment without extensive redesign efforts.

Beyond its technical expertise, Nijsha Enterprise has distinguished itself through a commitment to continuous improvement, compliance, and customer satisfaction. The company's dedication to **lean manufacturing principles, Six Sigma methodologies, and rigorous testing protocols** has ensured that every product it delivers meets the highest standards of quality and reliability. This reputation has not only earned the trust of government agencies such as the Department of Defense, NASA, and the Department of Energy but has also made

Nijsha a sought-after supplier in commercial markets ranging from automotive to medical device manufacturing.

By balancing innovation with disciplined execution, Nijsha Enterprise, Inc. has secured its position as an industry leader in cabling, printed circuit boards, wire harness production, and reverse engineering. The company's ability to bridge the gap between government and commercial contracting has provided a foundation for sustained growth, allowing Nijsha to expand its capabilities and forge new partnerships across industries. As the demand for high-performance electronic systems continues to rise, Nijsha remains committed to delivering cutting-edge solutions that meet the evolving needs of its clients while maintaining the highest levels of precision, reliability, and customer service.

8. **Continuous Learning and Adaptation**

Stay informed about industry trends, changes in government regulations, and new opportunities through continual learning. Resources such as webinars, industry reports, and government websites (e.g., SBA.gov) are invaluable for keeping your business strategies current and effective.

Starting as a small business in government contracting requires a practical and strategic approach, but it's certainly feasible with dedication and adaptability. By making the most of your existing resources, strategically outsourcing, and gradually building your capabilities, you can establish a strong foundation and grow your business sustainably in this competitive field.

Success in government contracting requires more than just winning contracts—it demands ongoing learning, adaptability, and strategic refinement. The federal procurement landscape is constantly evolving, shaped by shifts in government priorities, regulatory changes, technological advancements, and economic fluctuations. Contractors who remain static risk losing their competitive edge, while those who invest in continuous learning and adaptation position themselves for long-term sustainability and growth.

One of the most effective ways to stay ahead is by actively engaging with industry resources, regulatory updates, and professional development opportunities. Government agencies frequently revise procurement policies, modify compliance requirements, and introduce new initiatives that impact contracting opportunities. Keeping up with these changes through official government websites, industry publications, and professional networks ensures that businesses remain compliant and well-positioned to capitalize on emerging trends. The Small Business Administration (SBA.gov), Federal Acquisition Regulation (FAR) updates, and Defense Federal Acquisition Regulation Supplement (DFARS) amendments provide essential guidance on evolving requirements and best practices in federal contracting.

In addition to regulatory awareness, participating in industry webinars, attending conferences, and engaging in training programs are invaluable for continuous learning. Organizations such as the National Contract Management Association (NCMA), Government Contracting Academy, and Procurement Technical Assistance Centers (PTACs) offer specialized training designed to enhance business development strategies, compliance knowledge, and proposal writing skills. Webinars hosted by agencies such as the General Services Administration (GSA), Department of Defense (DoD), and Department of Homeland Security (DHS) provide direct insights into contracting opportunities, procurement forecasts, and policy changes.

Beyond formal training, networking with industry peers, mentors, and contracting officers fosters continuous learning through real-world experiences and best practice sharing. Attending roundtable discussions, business matchmaking events, and government-industry summits allows contractors to gain firsthand knowledge of challenges, solutions, and procurement expectations from seasoned professionals. Many successful government contractors also engage in mentor-protégé programs where they receive guidance from established businesses that have navigated the complexities of federal contracting. These relationships help smaller firms avoid common pitfalls and accelerate their learning curve.

Staying informed about market and industry trends is another critical aspect of continuous learning. Government spending priorities shift based on national security concerns, economic factors, and technological advancements. By analyzing industry reports, tracking contract award data, and leveraging market intelligence platforms such as GovWin, SAM.gov, and FPDS (Federal Procurement Data System), businesses can anticipate upcoming opportunities, refine their capture strategies, and tailor their offerings to meet government demands. Adapting to these trends allows businesses to remain relevant and competitive as federal procurement needs evolve.

Technology also plays a significant role in adaptation. The rise of artificial intelligence, automation, and cybersecurity requirements has changed how government agencies evaluate contractors. Businesses must continuously upgrade their capabilities, adopt emerging technologies, and implement digital transformation strategies to remain compliant with government expectations. For example, the Cybersecurity Maturity Model Certification (CMMC) framework now mandates strict cybersecurity standards for DoD contractors, requiring them to implement robust cybersecurity measures to protect sensitive government data. Contractors who proactively invest in compliance, cybersecurity infrastructure, and cloud-based collaboration tools not only mitigate risks but also gain a competitive edge when bidding on contracts.

Adaptation is not just about compliance and industry awareness—it also requires internal evaluation and process optimization. Businesses that conduct regular performance reviews, track key performance indicators (KPIs), and assess the effectiveness of their business strategies can make data-driven decisions that improve efficiency and profitability. Implementing lessons learned from previous contracts, refining proposal development processes, and adjusting pricing models based on competitive analysis ensure continuous improvement.

Finally, a mindset of flexibility and resilience is crucial in government contracting. Unexpected challenges—such as funding delays, contract modifications, or shifts in agency leadership—are common. Businesses that remain agile, pivot when necessary, and embrace change as part of the process are better equipped to sustain long-term success. This adaptability allows them to seize new opportunities, adjust to economic fluctuations, and maintain strong relationships with government clients despite external uncertainties.

Continuous learning and adaptation are not optional but essential for businesses that seek long-term viability and competitiveness in government contracting. By staying informed, investing in professional development, leveraging technology, optimizing business processes, and maintaining an adaptable mindset, companies can navigate the complexities of the federal marketplace, sustain growth, and secure future contract opportunities. Those who commit to this ongoing evolution will not only survive in the competitive world of government procurement but will thrive, building a legacy of success and innovation in the industry.

9. **Review and Adjustments:**

Throughout the capture and proposal development phases, various reviews (e.g., Pink Team, Red Team) are conducted to critique drafts and strategies. These reviews are crucial for identifying gaps, making necessary adjustments, and refining the approach to enhance the overall proposal quality.

Small businesses entering the government contracting space must be highly flexible, resourceful, and strategic when it comes to managing capture and proposal development. With limited personnel or some-times just a single owner handling multiple roles, these companies must adopt efficient processes that maximize their chances of securing contracts while maintaining operational sustainability. Unlike larger firms that have dedicated teams for business development, capture management, and proposal writing, small businesses must carefully balance these functions, often leveraging external support until they can gradually scale their internal resources.

At the outset, small businesses must take a methodical approach to proposal development. Many of the essential functions—market research, opportunity assessment, proposal writing, compliance review, and pricing strategy—must be managed with a lean staff. A single person may have to wear multiple hats, serving as the capture manager, proposal writer, pricing analyst, and compliance officer all at once. Given this reality, small businesses should prioritize investing in proposal management tools, outsourcing specialized tasks, and adopting a structured review process to improve efficiency and proposal quality.

One of the most effective ways for small businesses to bridge capability gaps is by contracting a company like Nijsha Enterprise, Inc., which specializes in capture management and proposal development. Engaging a firm with experience in federal contracting provides an opportunity to gain knowledge, refine skills, and understand the intricacies of proposal compliance without immediately hiring full-time staff. By working with an experienced team, small businesses can focus on building their technical and operational competencies while still being competitive in the bidding process.

The Role of Color Team Reviews in Proposal Development

Throughout the capture and proposal development phases, a series of structured color team reviews help refine strategy, identify weaknesses, and ensure that proposals are persuasive, compliant, and competitive

These reviews, commonly used by larger firms, are instrumental in producing high-quality proposals. However, small businesses may need to adapt these processes based on available resources, consolidating certain reviews to maintain efficiency.

- Blue Team Review focuses on the initial capture plan and draft proposal. This team ensures that the proposal aligns with the agency's mission, evaluates the competitive landscape, and identifies key differentiators that can strengthen the company's win strategy. For a small business, this review might be led by the business owner and a trusted external consultant, ensuring that the company's strategy is sound before further investment.
- Pink Team Review assesses content completeness, compliance, and initial argument structure after the first draft of the proposal is created. The goal is to check that all sections address the RFP requirements and that the value proposition is effectively communicated. In a small business, this may be conducted by a mentor, an outsourced proposal reviewer, or a teaming partner who can provide objective feedback.
- Red Team Review serves as the final comprehensive evaluation before submission. The reviewers examine the proposal from the government's perspective, ensuring that it is compelling, meets evaluation criteria, and clearly differentiates the company from competitors. Since small businesses often lack a full review team, a scaled-down "Red Team Lite" may be implemented using a third-party consultant or a senior industry expert to simulate a contracting officer's review process.
- Gold Team Review is the final pricing and risk assessment stage, where senior leadership evaluates the pricing strategy for competitiveness and profitability. For small businesses, this process is often handled by the owner or financial consultant, ensuring that pricing remains strategic yet realistic.

- White Team Review occurs post-submission and focuses on lessons learned to refine future proposals. Reviewing past performance, evaluating feedback from the government, and documenting areas for improvement ensures continuous learning.

Adapting Color Team Reviews for Small Businesses

While the color team review process is ideal for large firms, smaller businesses must tailor it to their resource constraints. A condensed version of these reviews allows small businesses to maintain quality control without overextending themselves.

- A Consolidated Review (Blue + Pink Team Combined) can be conducted after the first full draft of the proposal is completed. This single review should assess strategy, content completeness, compliance, and clarity. Business owners can engage an external consultant or teaming partner to provide fresh perspectives.
- A Final Review (Red Team Lite) should be done before submission, focusing on persuasiveness and compliance. This review can involve one or two trusted experts, such as an experienced contractor, consultant, or mentor who can analyze the proposal through the eyes of a contracting officer.
- A Post-Submission Reflection allows the small business to evaluate the entire proposal process and submission outcome. Gathering feedback internally and externally will help refine future proposals, ensuring continuous improvement and better positioning for upcoming opportunities.

Scaling Proposal Management as the Business Grows

As the company secures contracts and expands its capabilities, it can systematically add personnel to manage proposals. The first hires should be multi-skilled individuals who can handle both capture and proposal responsibilities, such as a business development specialist with proposal writing and compliance experience. Over time, as the company grows and pursues larger contracts, more specialized roles—such as a dedicated proposal manager, pricing analyst, and compliance officer—can be added.

Until a business is ready to build an in-house team, teaming with a company like Nijsha Enterprise, Inc. offers an ideal solution. Nijsha's expertise in proposal writing, compliance, and pricing strategy ensures that small businesses can submit competitive proposals while gaining hands-on experience. This approach allows small businesses to bid effectively, win contracts, and gradually build internal capabilities without overwhelming their resources.

Flexibility and strategic resource allocation are key to succeeding as a small business in government contracting. While a large team is not necessary at the outset, implementing an abbreviated proposal review process, leveraging external support, and carefully scaling personnel over time ensures that businesses can compete effectively. By adopting a structured approach, engaging industry experts, and continuously refining their proposal development process, small businesses can win government contracts, build credibility, and establish themselves as trusted providers in the federal marketplace.

CHAPTER 5
INTRODUCTION TO TIPS THAT QUALIFY A BUSINESS

The process of government contracting is elaborate and involves multiple strategic steps and considerations to ensure successful contract execution and compliance. Beginning with the critical step of holding a post-award conference, it is essential for both the government agency and the contractor to gain a mutual understanding of the contract's requirements. This conference helps identify and resolve potential issues early, setting the stage for a smooth project execution. If a contracting officer does not schedule this conference, it is prudent for contractors to request it to clarify performance expectations and discuss any uncertainties.

Preparation for the post-award conference involves assembling key personnel who understand the project's intricacies. This preparation ensures that all potential internal disagreements are addressed beforehand, and there is a clear strategy on how to present and negotiate details with government representatives. It's also beneficial to prepare an agenda that mirrors that of the agency to cover all critical points of discussion.

During the conference, it's advantageous to bring forward suggestions regarding how the government might assess and measure the project's outcomes. This proactive approach not only shows preparedness but also positions the contractor as a thoughtful and strategic partner. Ensuring all fundamental aspects of the contract such as communication practices, roles and responsibilities, and the specifics of deliverables and payments are thoroughly discussed and understood by both parties is crucial.

It is also essential to identify which government personnel will attend the conference and to align the contractor's representatives accordingly. If logistical issues prevent a physical meeting, proposing a virtual conference is a practical solution. Showing a proactive interest in the project's success from the start helps establish a positive working relationship with the government, which is beneficial for ongoing and future contracts.

Throughout the contract performance phase, maintaining an advantage through exemplary performance and understanding the broader contracting environment can lead to additional opportunities and contract renewals. Being vigilant about the performance metrics—such as timeliness, quality of product or service, and compliance with relevant regulations—ensures that the contractor meets or exceeds the government's expectations.

However, contractors must also be prepared for the potential misalignments between a contracting officer and their representative. Effective communication and documentation are vital in such scenarios to safeguard the contractor's interests and ensure clarity in contract execution. Understanding the authority and role of the contracting officer and their representatives helps prevent misunderstandings and contractual liabilities.

Contractors are required to provide access to their records for government audits, which ensures transparency and compliance with the contract terms. One of the unique aspects of government contracts is the possibility of changes by the contracting officer within the contract's scope, which the contractor must be prepared to accommodate, even if it requires additional resources.

The preparation and submission of an Equitable Adjustment request can arise if there are contract changes that incur extra costs. Understanding how to file claims and the subsequent processes, including potential appeals if a claim is denied, is crucial for contractors.

Ultimately, the contractor's performance is regularly evaluated, and these evaluations can significantly impact their reputation and future contract awards. Therefore, maintaining high standards in delivery, compliance, and customer service is paramount. Contractors have the opportunity to review and comment on performance assessments, which allows for ongoing improvements and accurate reflections of their performance.

In conclusion, navigating government contracts requires meticulous attention to detail, proactive management, and an understanding of the legal and operational frameworks. Contractors must remain agile, responsive, and compliant to succeed in this competitive arena. This comprehensive approach not only helps in fulfilling current contracts successfully but also paves the way for future opportunities in government contracting.

KEY TIPS TO HELP YOU

1. **Make sure there is a post-award conference.**

A Conference held promptly afterward will help both the government agency and the contractor achieve a clear, Mutual understanding of contract requirements in addition to providing an opportunity to identify and resolve any potential problems. If the Contracting officer isn't planning to hold a conference, the contractor should request one, especially if there's any doubt about what the government performance expectations are. A suggestion to conduct a debriefing inside. The post-award conference could be just the incentive that a contractor is looking to offer. A Contracting officer who is otherwise not inclined to hold a post-award orientation session.

2. **Prepare to attend the post-award conference.**

Conduct a pre-meeting involving your key personnel who will be involved in the fulfillment of the contract. Any differences of opinion among one another should be reconciled, and there should be an iron-clad understanding about who the contractor's chief spokesperson is and how the meeting will be conducted with government Representatives. Ask for the agency's agenda and prepare your agenda as well to ensure that everything important to your interest is covered during the meeting.

3. **Bring suggestions to the post-award conference.**

Make recommendations at the conference about the assessment, measurement, and surveillance standards that you think would be reasonable for the government to use in judging the adequacy of your contract performance. Making suggestions about these factors during the post- award conference will serve your interest. And will most likely be welcomed by government officials.

4. **Make sure key points are covered in the post-award conference.**

At a minimum, make sure this is covered:

- Communications Practices between agency and contractor personnel, as well as the contract Administration process.
- Responsibilities of the parties.
- Post award Communications.
- Deliverables and progress reports.
- All terms deal with deliverables, acceptance, and payment.
- See DD Form 1484 for more possible topics.

5. **Find out in advance what government Personnel will be in attendance at the post-award conference.**

When to bring corresponding members of your team. Make sure one of your team members takes minutes of the conference so that you can compare notes at the end of the meeting. If distance, travel, or cost are impediments to holding a post-award conference, suggest a teleconference or a WebEx meeting format.

6. **Display interest in good performance at the outset.**

A contractor who does this is on track to establishing a good relationship with the government. Remember, the government needs solutions, and you are the solution provider. You should work throughout the term of every contract on establishing positive relationships with the government people who play a role in the Contracting process. These people include the Contracting officer and Contracting officers' representative, to be sure, but also include the end-user and agency small business officer.

7. **During the contract performance, exploit the incumbency advantage. incumbents that perform well, display a helpful attitude, and demonstrate an understanding of the Government Contracting environment. It does increase the odds that their contract options are exercised and that they receive new contract Awards.**

8. **Be aware of the performance categories most often measured and a government contract.**

They are:

- Delivery/schedule (timeliness).
- Product/service quality.
- Business relations.
- Management of key personnel.
- Customer satisfaction.
- Compliance, for example: occupational safety and health administration OSHA rules, Environmental Protection Agency EPA rules, labor laws, small business subcontracting plan.

9. **Be vigilant about the possibility that the Contracting officer and the Contracting officer representative may not always be in sync.**

Contracting Representatives verify the contractor's compliance with documents and validate a contract completion. They identify performance indicators and provide a written report to the Contracting officer, including any performance deficiencies. The Contracting officer and the Contracting officer representative must establish a good working Rapport and open Communications, or contractors should be alert to the possibility that this is not always the case. When the Contracting officer and the Contracting officer representative are not in sync, the contractor, to protect its interests, will need to be vigilant and document any differences and the direction being received from the two parties.

10. **Always remember the authority of the Contracting officer and the Contracting officer's representative.**

Only the Contracting officer can direct a contractor to take an action not in the contract that will cause the government to incur additional cost. A Contracting officer's representative who fails to maintain good Communications with the Contracting officer. Because of an experience or lack of training, sometimes the Contracting officers Representatives unknowingly exceed the limits of their Authority. This can cause potential liability for the government and contractual uncertainties for both the government and the contractor.

11. **Recognize that the government Auditors have a right to look at your records.**

Contractors are obligated to provide to the government documents, accounting procedures and practices, and other data, regardless of if these items are in paper or electronic form, along with supporting

ocumentation to satisfy contract negotiation and administration. It's a
ontract violation to deny and not provide records in a timely manner.
ypically, to resolve issues, they may want to look at actual documents,
ach as original purchase orders, invoices, receipts, timesheets, ledgers,
nd other financial documents.

2. **Be aware of one of the most unique features of a government contract: A Contracting officer may at any time make changes within the general scope of a contract.**

he contractor is obligated to perform the work before an actual price
djustment in the form of a formal contract modification is negotiated.
s long as the changed work is within the scope of the original
ontract, it should be accommodated by the contractor. Even though
hanges may require added resources. The government has the power
o direct that a change be made even over a contractor's objection, but
ae government cannot modify a contract so that it is materially
ifferent from the original contract.

3. **Know that a contract change order the government makes that causes a contractor to do something.**

his is known as a constructive change. Sometimes, this creates the
eed for a call to the contracting officer. It depends on the situation of
 contract. By contacting the Contracting officer this results in an extra
xpense with the contractor. Similarly, a defective specification can still
vork when the contractor relies on a government representation that
roves to be accurate. Not recognizing the extra work involved, the
orrecting officer may refuse to pay for it. Unless resolved locally, the
Determination that a constructive change has occurred may need to
e made by an agency or the contractor appeals or by the court,
hereby authorizing payment for the extra cost incurred by the
ontractor.

14. **Understand what a request for an Equitable adjustment (REA) is.**

A Rea is initiated when a contractor calls the contracting law office's attention to a contract problem. The contract officer may ask the contractor to put in writing a description of the problem and a dollar estimate to take care of it. When this is put in writing it should be labeled a request for an Equitable adjustment. If the Contracting officer believes the request for Equitable adjustment is appropriate, the Contracting officer can move to solve the issue, including negotiating the amount of money needed. It's a contract that grieves; both parties can agree to modify the contract without a claim ever being filed.

15. **Understand what a claim is and how to file one.**

There are several elements to a client. The claim must include a description of the contract problem that serves as the basis for the claim, the solution and a corresponding demand for a specific sum of money, and a demand for a final decision by the Contracting officer. In addition, if the money being demanded is more than $100,000, the contractor must certify the claim. The language for doing that can be found in the dispute Clause of the contract.

16. **Understand the rules when firing a client.**

The Government Contracting officer has 60 days to issue a final decision on a claim. If the contracting officer does not meet this deadline, the contractor can't consider the life of a decision to be a denial and, thus, proceed to file an appeal to the agency's board of contract Appeals. Or to the District Court of federal claims. It's important to note that these bodies review the claim. Denovo without regard to the Contracting officer's final decision. This means that if the Contracting officer's final decision resulted in the award of a sum of money, a bad decision could result in an award for more or less. There is one fina stage of appeal, to the federal court of appeals. That appeal is not de novo.

17. **Be aware of what the government may do if they find your performance unsatisfactory.**

- Depending on a Contracting officer's evaluation of the seriousness of the unsatisfactory performance, he or she may do the following:
- Bring the deficiency to the attention of a contractor by a letter or through a meeting, with the objective of a painting. A commitment for appropriate corrective action.
- Extend the contract schedule if excusable delays and performance are involved, such as combat situations or extreme weather conditions.
- Withhold contract payments if a contractor fails to comply with the delivery or reporting provisions of the contract.
- Terminate the contract for cause or default.

18. **Know what you should do if you receive a notice of a performance failure.**

Respond immediately. It's a big mistake to brush off or to not take seriously any negative feedback from a contractor officer or Contracting officer representative. It's much wiser to respond quickly, conveying an attitude of willingness to make things right. Procrastination to respond will only make things worse and give evidence to the government that you are not concerned with performance. Then, address the deficiencies and invite Government Representatives for a review. Redo if necessary. If a contractor is interested in a government sector business for the Long Haul, responsiveness can't turn lemons into lemonade.

19. **Know what to do if there's a problem the government doesn't know about.**

No one likes to be a bearer of bad news, but when performing a contract, it is better to fess up early than let a problem Fester. Usually, the Government Contracting team will appreciate it when they are contracted as forthcoming about a problem, that way, both parties can work together to remedy a situation which will likely only thing work that the left under. To be sure, one of the ways our situation can get worse. Lateral Lamborghinis imposed by the government on the contractor. These remedies can be avoided or Millikan way through forthcoming communication early problem identification by the contractor.

20. **If you are selling a commercial item to the government, know that the government will rely on your account. Tender for acceptance of forms to the contract.**

This is generally appropriate when the government is a shirring non-conflict commercial item. Remember, though. The government always has the right to refuse acceptance of non-conforming items.

21. **Know that acceptance is ordinarily evidence by execution of an accurate certificate on an inspection or receiving Report Form or on a commercial chicken document packing list.**

It may be in the government's interest to simply accept supplies or services on the basis of the contractor's certificate of conformance. Examples of this include situations in which only a small loss will be incurred in the event of a defect, or because of the contractors reputation or passport, It is likely that the supplies or Services furnished will be acceptable and any defensive work will be replaced. Look for appropriate form in your contract or inquire.

22. **Be aware of the fact that the government is entitled to what is called "strict compliance " with the technical requirements of the contract.**

This means the service or hide them actually furnished under a contract must be equal to or superior to that described in the contract specifications. Strict compliance means exactly that, and there are serious risk for non-compliance. While the government took the lead does not establish elaborate contract monitoring plan when purchasing commercial products or Services, the other meant none Deluxe always we change the right to perform inspection and acceptance in any contract.

23. **Look in your contract document to find the government office responsible for payment plan to find the invoice and instructions.**

Follow those instructions carefully because the more accurate and invoice you submit, the more quickly you will be paid. If the government fails to make payment on a properly prepared invoice, the government is obligated to pay an interest penalty.

24. **Understand what may be the most unique feature of a government contract. . The government made unilaterally terminate your contract or convenience if it is in the government's interest to do so.**

The reasons for a termination for convenience usually involve:

- There is no longer a need for the item or service or the quantity needed has been reduced as cold for under the contract.
- Funds are not available for continued contract performance, or there has been a radical change in the needs of

government that goes well beyond the scope of the current contract.

25. **Know what the government's alternatives to contract termination are.**

- Continuing the present contract by revising the schedule or permitting the contractor to subcontract.
- Choosing delivery or other requirement and obtaining compensation from the contractor and return.
- Modifying part of the contract for cause or default.
- Modifying part of the contract for convenience.

When faced with a significant change and requirements, Alternatives may include:

- Canceling a purchase order not yet accepted by the contractor. Permitting the contractor to complete the current contract, because it is more cost-effective and terminated for convenience.
- Issuing a no-cost cancellation when: The supply or service can be readily obtained elsewhere. A no cost settlement is acceptable to the contractor.

26. **Know that the government must pay for the privilege of terminating a contract for convenience and compensate the contractor for this action.**

If properly documented and supported, costs can include:

- Startup cost.
- Unexpired leases and leasehold, Improvements.
- Specialized equipment required to perform the contract.
- Severance and outplacement expenses.

- Expenses associated with the protection, preservation and disposition of government property and inventory.
- Expenses associated with the protection, preservation and disposition of government property and inventory.
- Cost to prepare a termination settlement proposal, and Prophet on work completed, and other costs.

This is one time where overhead cost may be billed as direct course. Settlement, expenses and include accounting, legal, and clerical course. Indirect costs related to Valerie and wages incurred as settlement expenses can be included as well.

27. **If your contract is terminated, know what you are obligated to do.**

- Stop working immediately.
- If you stop work and termination notices to subcontractors.
- Meet with Subs to clarify requirements and answer questions.
- Control an account for all government-owned property, including any in the possession of subcontractors.
- Established cost collection code to segregate and accumulate allowable costs in cured subsequent to termination.
- Established a new project reference number or change code to capture these allowable costs in cured after termination, labor and other costs separately from the actual contract work.
- Assess the status of the Prime contract and subcontract for any undefinitized change orders.
- Complete the government for quiet schedule of accounting information, SF 1439, for each termination for which a settlement proposal is submitted.

28. **If your contract is terminated, know what you should do to protect your interest.**

- Established a settlement account and budget.
- Create an estimate of completion.
- Push for action on unfunded work and REA's.
- Conduct an Inventory.
- Obtain settlement proposals from subcontractors and terminate any other arrangements.
- Be aware of deadlines, forms, and appropriate cost principles that apply.
- Remember that settlement can be based on compromise.
- Request settlement cost be paid on an interim basis.
- Be aware that the truth in negotiations Act (TINA) applies.
- No, there are limits on the cost of re- procurement.

29. **Be aware that government agencies are obligated to collect information and report on contractor performance.**

Rules require agencies to prepare an evaluation of contractor performance on each contract in excess of $150,000, but performance report may be prepared or contract of any value. This information is used in future Source elections. Generally, these reports contain ratings of contractors in four categories.

- Quality of the product or service provided.
- Ability to control cost.
- Ability to meet schedule,
- And quality of business relations such as customer service.

30. **Know that you can review and comment on the reports the government creates about your contract performance.**

The contractor performance assessment reporting system (CPARS) allows contractors to electronically submit comments regarding the government assessment and to indicate concurrent or Naga college with the overall evaluation. A senior agency official is to review each government contractor's disagreement to ensure that the final report reflects a fair evaluation.

Government Contracting matters.

It is a very sobering feeling to be up in space and realize that one safety factor was determined by the lowest bidder on a government contract.

Here is a table summarizing all 30 tips for navigating government contracting successfully:

Tip Number	Key Tip Summary
1	**Post-Award Conference:** Ensure a conference is held to clarify contract requirements and expectations. If not scheduled, request one.
2	**Preparation for Post-Award Conference:** Prepare by reconciling internal opinions and understanding the agency's agenda.
3	**Suggestions at Post-Award Conference:** Bring forward suggestions on assessment and surveillance standards that might be adopted.
4	**Key Points at Post-Award Conference:** Cover communication practices, roles, progress reports, and terms of deliverables and payments.
5	**Identify Government Personnel:** Know who will attend from the government side; prepare accordingly and plan for virtual alternatives if needed.
6	**Show Interest in Performance:** Establish a good relationship from the start by showing proactive engagement and understanding of government needs.
7	**Exploit the Incumbency Advantage:** Use your position to better understand the contracting environment and increase the likelihood of future contracts.
8	**Performance Categories:** Be aware of commonly measured performance categories like timeliness, quality, and compliance.
9	**Contracting Officer Synchronization:** Ensure good communication with the Contracting officer and their representative; document any discrepancies.
10	**Authority of Contracting Officer:** Understand the limits of the Contracting officer's authority, especially regarding cost-related directives.

11   **Government Auditors' Rights:** Be prepared to show records and documentation to government auditors to verify compliance and contract execution.

12   **Contract Modifications:** Be prepared to accommodate changes within the contract scope as directed by the Contracting officer.

13   **Constructive Changes:** Understand what constitutes a constructive change and how it might impact cost and contract execution.

14   **Equitable Adjustments (REA):** Know how to request an REA if changes cause unexpected expenses or contractual challenges.

15   **Understanding Claims:** Learn how to file a claim, including what information must be included and the process for doing so.

16   **Rules When Firing a Client:** Understand the procedures and timelines if you need to file a claim due to unresolved issues.

17   **Unsatisfactory Performance Actions:** Know the potential government actions if performance is deemed unsatisfactory, including contract termination.

18   **Responding to Performance Failures:** Always respond promptly to negative feedback or performance evaluations to demonstrate commitment to improvement.

19   **Handling Undisclosed Problems:** Proactively report and address any problems not yet known to the government to foster transparency and trust.

20   **Selling Commercial Items:** Be aware of the government's reliance on contractor provided forms and the right to refuse non-conforming items.

21   **Acceptance of Items:** Understand the processes for government acceptance of supplies or services, including the significance of compliance certificates.

22   **Strict Compliance Requirement:** Be prepared to meet or exceed the technical specifications as detailed in the contract.

23   **Invoice and Payment Processes:** Know where to find payment instructions in your contract documents and comply meticulously to ensure prompt payment.

24   **Contract Termination for Convenience:** Recognize the government's right to terminate a contract for convenience and know the implications.

25   **Alternatives to Contract Termination:** Understand the various alternatives to termination and how they might be used to adjust contract terms.

26   **Compensation for Termination:** Be aware that compensation for termination for convenience must cover all relevant costs as documented.

27   **Obligations Upon Contract Termination:** Know your immediate obligations if a contract is terminated, including stopping work and accounting for government property.

28   **Protecting Interests Post-Termination:** Establish protocols for managing termination, including settling accounts and pursuing compensation.

29   **Contractor Performance Reporting:** Be aware of the requirement for performance evaluations and how they can impact future contracting opportunities.

30   **Reviewing Performance Reports:** Take the opportunity to review and comment on performance reports to ensure they fairly reflect your work.

This table serves as a comprehensive guide for contractors navigating the complexities of government contracts, providing a quick reference to essential practices that support successful contract management and execution.

HELPFUL WEB RESOURCES

Federal Acquisition Regulation:
Https://farsite.hill.af.mil

Guide to Best Practices for Contract Administration
www. Acquisition.gov/bestpractices/bestpcont.html

Post Award Conference Record:
http://tinyurl.com/bvpndnq

Manual for Contractors Defense Contract Audit Agency:
www. Dacc.mil/cam. Html

Contractor Performance Assessment Reporting Agency
www. cpars.gov

Contacting News and Educational Opportunities :
www.contractingacademy.gatech.edu

Feel free to contact us about our Mentorship Educational Program and Online Webinar
Classes

Nijsha Enterprise Inc
The Support of Global Industries
Web: www. Nijshaenterprise.com
Email: Jerrell@nijshaenterprise.com or nijsha@att.net

Kevin Harrington original member from the Hit TV series Shark Tank, interviewed & endorsed the President & CEO of Nijsha Enterprise Jerrell Johnson Jr. The interview was aired on Fox TV nationally.

APPENDIX A: GLOSSARY

Affirmative Action Plan (AAP) – A requirement for federal contractors to establish equal employment opportunity programs, ensuring nondiscrimination in hiring and employment practices.

Alternative Dispute Resolution (ADR) – A process used to resolve disputes outside of court, including mediation and arbitration, often employed in government contracting disputes.

Anti-Deficiency Act (ADA) – A federal law prohibiting government officials from obligating or spending more than the amounts available in appropriations or funds.

Audit Trail: Documentation that traces the detailed transactions relating to financial data, contract management, and compliance, used to verify the legitimacy of transactions and in forensic investigations.

Authorized Negotiator – An individual listed in a contractor's System for Award Management (SAM) registration who is legally permitted to discuss and modify contract terms with the government.

Award Fee Contract – A type of cost-reimbursement contract where the government provides an incentive fee based on performance.

Best Value Procurement: A method that emphasizes value over cost, where the government looks at factors such as performance risk and contractor reliability in addition to price.

Bid Protest – A formal challenge filed with the Government Accountability Office (GAO) or another agency, disputing the award or terms of a government contract.

Billing Rate Agreement – A negotiated agreement between a contractor and the government that establishes predetermined labor and overhead rates for billing purposes.

Blanket Purchase Agreement (BPA): An arrangement between the government and a vendor that allows for the repeated purchase of supplies or services at set prices, streamlining the process for frequent needs.

Blue Team Review: An initial review to validate the capture strategy and the alignment of the proposal's approach with strategic goals.

Buy American Act (BAA) – A regulation requiring federal contractors to use American-made materials and goods unless an exception applies.

Capture Management: Process involving strategic steps from deciding to pursue a government contract to the release of the RFP, aimed at increasing the win probability.

Change Management: The process of managing changes to the contract scope, often involving negotiations for equitable adjustments in terms of time and cost.

Change Order – A formal directive from the Contracting Officer modifying the terms, conditions, or scope of work under an existing contract.

Claim – A formal request submitted by a contractor to a contracting officer for additional compensation or time due to unforeseen contract changes or issues.

Competitive Bidding: The process by which the government invites multiple firms to submit bids on a project, with the contract being awarded to the firm that meets the technical criteria at the lowest price or best value.

Conflict of Interest: Situations where personal interests of an individual involved in the contracting process could potentially or actually conflict with the best interests of the government.

Constructive Change: A change order that is not formally issued but occurs due to government action, leading to additional costs for the contractor.

Contract Award Notice: An official announcement made by the government agency indicating that a contract has been awarded to a particular bidder.

Contract Award: The decision by the government to grant a contract to a particular bidder based on the evaluation of proposals.

Contract Compliance: Adherence to the terms, conditions, and regulatory requirements of the contract as outlined in the agreement between the government and the contractor.

Contract Data Requirements List (CDRL) – A list within a government contract that specifies deliverable reports, documentation, and data submission deadlines.

Contract Disputes Act (CDA) – The law governing how disputes between federal contractors and government agencies are handled, including appeal rights.

Contract Execution: The phase where the work specified in the contract is performed and managed according to the contractual obligations agreed upon by both parties.

Contract Lifecycle: The complete phase of a contract from initiation and award, through management and compliance, to closure or termination.

Contract Line Item Number (CLIN) – A unique identifier assigned to specific goods or services within a contract, helping track performance and invoicing.

Contract Modification: Adjustments within the general scope of the contract initiated by the contracting officer, requiring contractor compliance.

Contract Performance Assessment Reporting System (CPARS) – A government database used to record and evaluate contractor performance, impacting future bid evaluations.

Contract Termination for Convenience: The government's right to unilaterally terminate a contract when it serves their interest, regardless of the contractor's performance.

Contracting Authority: The official capacity granted to specific individuals, such as Contracting Officers, to enter into, administer, or terminate contracts and make related determinations and findings.

Contracting Officer: The authorized individual who can legally bind the government in contracts and direct significant contract changes that affect cost.

Contracting Officer's Representative (COR): Assigned by the contracting officer to ensure proper contract performance and compliance but cannot change contract terms affecting cost.

Contractor Purchasing System Review (CPSR) – A government audit of a contractor's procurement policies and practices to ensure compliance with federal regulations.

Cost Accounting Standards (CAS) – A set of 19 financial regulations imposed on larger federal contracts to ensure consistency and transparency in cost accounting.

Cost Analysis: A detailed examination and evaluation of each cost element within a proposal, including labor, materials, overhead, and profit, ensuring that the overall price offered by the contractor is fair and reasonable.

Cost Reimbursement Contract: A type of contract where the contractor is paid for all allowed expenses to a set limit plus additional payment to allow for a profit.

Cost-Reimbursement Contract – A contract where the government reimburses allowable costs incurred by the contractor, with or without an additional fixed fee.

Covered Defense Information (CDI) – Sensitive but unclassified defense-related information that requires protection under federal cybersecurity regulations.

CPARS (Contractor Performance Assessment Reporting System): A system used by the government to rate and record contractor performance, affecting future contract awards.

Cumulative Allowable Cost Worksheet (CACW) – A required financial document submitted with incurred cost proposals to ensure accurate contract cost tracking.

DD Form 1484: A form used in government contracting to document specific aspects of the contract, often referenced in discussions about deliverables and payments.

Debriefing: A session offered by the government to bidders after the award decision is made, providing feedback on their proposals to aid in future submissions.

Defective Pricing – Occurs when a contractor fails to submit accurate, current, and complete pricing data, violating the Truth in Negotiations Act (TINA).

Defense Contract Audit Agency (DCAA) – The agency responsible for auditing financial records of government contractors to ensure compliance with federal cost principles.

Defense Federal Acquisition Regulation Supplement (DFARS) – A supplement to the FAR that governs the Department of Defense's procurement policies and contract requirements.

Definitive Contract – A contract that is finalized with agreed-upon terms, scope, and price after negotiations are completed.

Delivery Order (DO) – An order placed against an existing indefinite delivery contract (such as an IDIQ) for specified goods or services.

Delivery Order: An order typically used for acquiring goods, where the quantity and delivery requirements are specified in the contract.

Determination and Findings (D&F) – A written justification by the government for making an unusual contract decision, such as awarding a sole-source contract.

Due Diligence: The comprehensive appraisal of a business undertaken by a prospective buyer, especially to establish its assets and liabilities and evaluate its commercial potential in contract negotiations.

Economic Price Adjustment (EPA) Clause – A contract provision allowing for price adjustments based on inflation, market conditions, or changes in labor costs.

Equitable Adjustment (REA): A financial adjustment requested by a contractor to cover costs incurred due to contract changes or other conditions impacting performance.

Ethics in Contracting: A set of moral principles that guide the behaviors and decisions of those involved in government contracting, ensuring fairness, transparency, and integrity throughout the procurement process.

Federal Acquisition Regulations (FAR): The primary set of rules in the Federal Acquisition Regulation system that governs the government procurement process.

Federal Business Opportunities (FBO.gov) – The previous government contracting website replaced by SAM.gov for posting solicitations and contract awards.

Federal Contract Compliance Programs (FCCP) – The Department of Labor program ensuring government contractors follow equal employment opportunity laws.

Federal Financial Assistance – Grants, cooperative agreements, or other funding mechanisms awarded to non-federal entities for specified purposes.

Federal Information Security Modernization Act (FISMA) – A regulation requiring federal agencies and contractors to implement cybersecurity measures to protect government information.

Federal Supply Schedule (FSS): A program directed and managed by the General Services Administration (GSA) that provides federal agencies with a simplified process of acquiring commercial supplies and services at prices associated with volume buying.

Firm Fixed Price Level of Effort (FFP-LOE) – A contract type where the contractor is paid a fixed amount based on delivering a specified level of effort rather than a final product.

Fixed-Price Contract: A contract where the contractor is paid a set amount regardless of incurred expenses, emphasizing cost control and efficient performance.

Foreign Military Sales (FMS) – A program allowing U.S. defense contractors to sell military equipment and services to allied nations with government approval.

Full and Open Competition: A procurement principle under which all responsible sources are allowed to submit a bid, proposal, or quote, promoting fair and competitive contracting practices.

General and Administrative (G&A) Costs – Indirect costs that support overall business operations but are not directly tied to contract performance.

Gold Team Review: A review that focuses on pricing and the decision to proceed with the proposal submission based on its competitiveness and compliance.

Government Auditors: Professionals tasked with reviewing and ensuring the contractor's financial and operational adherence to the contract terms.

Government-Wide Acquisition Contract (GWAC) – A long-term contract vehicle allowing multiple agencies to procure IT products and services from pre-approved vendors.

Incremental Funding – A contract funding method where the government obligates funds in phases rather than providing full funding upfront.

Incremental Funding: A method of funding contracts that provides specific amounts of money at designated times, rather than full funding from the start of the contract.

Incumbency Advantage: The competitive edge current contract holders have, derived from their established performance history and relationship with the contracting agency.

Incurred Cost Submission (ICS) – A required annual financial report for cost-reimbursement contracts, detailing actual expenses incurred.

Indefinite Delivery, Indefinite Quantity (IDIQ) Contract – A contract that provides flexibility in ordering goods or services over a fixed period without specifying exact quantities upfront.

Indefinite Delivery, Indefinite Quantity (IDIQ) Contract: A type of contract that provides for an indefinite quantity of supplies or services during a fixed period, with deliveries or performance to be scheduled by placing orders with the contractor.

Labor Hour (LH) Contract – A variation of time-and-materials contracts where payment is based on labor hours performed at fixed hourly rates.

Material Cost Allowability – The regulations governing which material costs can be billed under a federal contract.

Micro-Purchase Threshold (MPT) – The dollar limit under which federal agencies can make purchases without formal solicitation requirements, currently set at $10,000.

Milestone Payments: Payments made to the contractor upon reaching predefined stages or achievements in the project, encouraging progress and providing ongoing working capital.

Most Favored Customer Pricing (MFC) – A pricing requirement where contractors must offer the government the same or better pricing as their best commercial customers.

Negotiated Procurement: A method of procurement where terms, conditions, and possibly the final price are modified before contract award through negotiation.

Negotiation Memorandum: A document that records the discussions, negotiations, and rationale for decisions made during contract negotiations between the government and the contractor.

Notice to Proceed (NTP) – A formal notification issued by the government directing the contractor to begin contract performance.

Office of Federal Procurement Policy (OFPP) – The government office that establishes procurement policies to improve efficiency, competition, and cost-effectiveness in federal acquisitions.

Past Performance Information Retrieval System (PPIRS) – A government database used to track contractor performance history, now integrated into CPARS.

Performance Assessment: The evaluation process conducted by the government to assess the contractor's performance against the contractual standards and requirements.

Performance Bond: A bond issued by a bank or insurance company to guarantee satisfactory completion of a project by a contractor, providing a financial assurance that the contractor will perform all obligations under the contract.

Performance Categories: Specific areas in which the government assesses the contractor's performance, including quality, timeliness, and compliance.

Performance Failure Notice: Notification from the contracting officer detailing performance issues, requiring immediate corrective action by the contractor.

Performance Metrics: Specific criteria used to measure and evaluate the efficiency, effectiveness, and compliance of the work performed by the contractor.

Pink Team Review: A preliminary review of the proposal draft focusing on content and alignment with the RFP requirements.

Post-Award Conference: A meeting conducted after contract award to clarify requirements and expectations between the government and the contractor.

Prompt Payment Act (PPA) – A law requiring federal agencies to pay contractors in a timely manner and outlining penalties for late payments.

Proposal Compliance Matrix: A tool used to align proposal responses with the requirements of the RFP, ensuring all aspects of the request are adequately addressed.

Proposal Development: The process of creating a proposal in response to an RFP, detailing how the contractor will meet the government's requirements.

Qualifications-Based Selection (QBS): A procurement process used, particularly in professional services contracts, where the selection is based on qualifications and competence rather than price.

Red Team Review: A critical, final review of the proposal before submission, aimed at ensuring it is compelling and error-free.

Request for Information (RFI): A formal request sent out by the government to gather information about the capabilities of various vendors before issuing an RFP.

RFP (Request for Proposal): A document issued by the government to invite contractors to submit a proposal for the delivery of goods or services.

Risk Management: The systematic process of identifying, analyzing, and responding to project risks to minimize the impact on the project.

Scope Creep: The uncontrolled expansion to project scope without adjustments to time, cost, and resources, typically requiring careful management and contractual adjustments.

Sealed Bidding – A procurement method where contractors submit sealed bids, and the lowest responsible bidder is awarded the contract.

Service Contract Act (SCA) – A labor law requiring contractors to pay prevailing wages and benefits to employees working on federal service contracts.

Simplified Acquisition Procedures (SAP) – A streamlined procurement method for contracts under a certain dollar threshold to reduce administrative burden.

Small Disadvantaged Business (SDB) – A federal designation for small businesses owned by socially and economically disadvantaged individuals.

Solicitation Document: An official request issued by a government agency that invites entities to submit bids or proposals for the supply of goods and services.

Source Selection: The process used by government agencies to evaluate proposals and choose the most suitable vendor based on established criteria outlined in the RFP.

Strict Compliance: Requirement for services or goods delivered to meet or exceed all technical specifications outlined in the contract.

Subcontracting Plan: A formal plan that outlines how the prime contractor aims to involve subcontractors, particularly small businesses and other socio-economic categories.

Task Order: An order for services placed against an established contract or with government sources, specifying tasks to be performed and associated details.

Technical Evaluation: A thorough review and assessment of a contractor's technical proposal to ensure it meets the specific technical and operational requirements outlined in the RFP.

Termination for Default: The government's right to terminate a contract due to the contractor's failure to comply with contractual terms.

TINA (Truth in Negotiations Act): Legislation requiring cost or pricing data to be accurate, complete, and current for negotiations of contracts above a certain threshold.

Total Evaluated Price (TEP) – The final price used by government evaluators to compare bids, factoring in cost, incentives, and discounts.

Unsatisfactory Performance: Evaluation by the contracting officer that a contractor's performance does not meet contractual standards or expectations.

APPENDIX B: ABBREVIATIONS AND ACRONYMS

Government contracting involves extensive use of abbreviations and acronyms. Understanding these terms is essential for effective communication and compliance with federal procurement requirements. Below is a comprehensive list of commonly used abbreviations and acronyms in the government contracting industry.

A

AAP – Affirmative Action Plan

ADA – Anti-Deficiency Act

ADR – Alternative Dispute Resolution

AID – Agency for International Development

AO – Administrative Officer

AOR – Administrative Officer's Representative

APO – Authorized Procurement Officer

ARRA – American Recovery and Reinvestment Act

ASBCA – Armed Services Board of Contract Appeals

B

BAA – Buy American Act

BPA – Blanket Purchase Agreement

BOS – Business Operations Support

BOA – Basic Ordering Agreement

BOE – Basis of Estimate

BPA – Blanket Purchase Agreement

C

CAGE – Commercial and Government Entity (Code)

CAO – Contract Administration Office

CAS – Cost Accounting Standards

CBA – Cost-Benefit Analysis

CBD – Commerce Business Daily (Replaced by SAM.gov)

CBP – Customs and Border Protection

CDA – Contract Disputes Act

CDRL – Contract Data Requirements List

CFR – Code of Federal Regulations

CICA – Competition in Contracting Act

CIO – Chief Information Officer

CLIN – Contract Line Item Number

CO – Contracting Officer

COA – Course of Action

CONUS – Continental United States

COR – Contracting Officer's Representative

COTS – Commercial Off-the-Shelf

CPARS – Contractor Performance Assessment Reporting System

CPFF – Cost-Plus-Fixed-Fee

CPIF – Cost-Plus-Incentive-Fee

CPI – Contractor Performance Index

CPSR – Contractor Purchasing System Review

D

D&F – Determination and Findings

DCAA – Defense Contract Audit Agency

DHS – Department of Homeland Security

DIA – Defense Intelligence Agency

DLA – Defense Logistics Agency

DOD – Department of Defense

DOE – Department of Energy

DOI – Department of the Interior

DOT – Department of Transportation

DPAS – Defense Priorities and Allocations System

DUNS – Data Universal Numbering System (Replaced by UEI - Unique Entity Identifier)

DVBE – Disabled Veteran Business Enterprise

DFARS – Defense Federal Acquisition Regulation Supplement

E

ECP – Engineering Change Proposal

EDA – Electronic Document Access

EEO – Equal Employment Opportunity

EPA – Economic Price Adjustment

EPLS – Excluded Parties List System (Now part of SAM.gov)

ESC – Evaluation Support Contractor

EVMS – Earned Value Management System

F

F&A – Facilities and Administrative Costs

FAPIIS – Federal Awardee Performance and Integrity Information System

FAR – Federal Acquisition Regulation

FBO – Federal Business Opportunities (Now SAM.gov)

FCA – False Claims Act

FCL – Facility Clearance Level

FFP – Firm-Fixed-Price

FISMA – Federal Information Security Modernization Act

FMS – Foreign Military Sales

FOIA – Freedom of Information Act

FPI – Fixed-Price Incentive

FSRS – Federal Subaward Reporting System

G

GAO – Government Accountability Office

G&A – General and Administrative

GFE – Government-Furnished Equipment

GFP – Government-Furnished Property

GPC – Government Purchase Card

GSA – General Services Administration

GWAC – Government-Wide Acquisition Contract

H

HBCU – Historically Black Colleges and Universities

HUBZone – Historically Underutilized Business Zone

I

IAW – In Accordance With

ID/IQ – Indefinite Delivery/Indefinite Quantity

IFB – Invitation for Bid

IGCE – Independent Government Cost Estimate

INC – Incorporated

INS – Immigration and Naturalization Service

IPT – Integrated Product Team

ISR – Individual Subcontract Report

J

J&A – Justification and Approval

K

KO – Contracting Officer

L

LOE – Level of Effort

LPTA – Lowest Price Technically Acceptable

M

M&O – Management and Operating Contract

MOU – Memorandum of Understanding

MPT – Micro-Purchase Threshold

N

NAICS – North American Industry Classification System

NASA – National Aeronautics and Space Administration

NDAA – National Defense Authorization Act

NITAAC – National Institutes of Health Information Technology Acquisition and Assessment Center

O

O&M – Operations and Maintenance

OCI – Organizational Conflict of Interest

OFPP – Office of Federal Procurement Policy

OMB – Office of Management and Budget

P

PALT – Procurement Administrative Lead Time

P-Card – Purchase Card

PEO – Program Executive Office

PIA – Procurement Integrity Act

PMP – Project Management Plan

PPA – Prompt Payment Act

PPIRS – Past Performance Information Retrieval System (Now CPARS)

P-Win – Probability of Win

Q

QASP – Quality Assurance Surveillance Plan

QBS – Qualifications-Based Selection

R

R&D – Research and Development

RFI – Request for Information

RFP – Request for Proposal

RFQ – Request for Quotation

RMP – Risk Management Plan

S

SABER – Simplified Acquisition of Base Engineering Requirements

SAM – System for Award Management

SBA – Small Business Administration

SBD – Small Business Development

SCA – Service Contract Act

SDVOSB – Service-Disabled Veteran-Owned Small Business

SEWP – Solutions for Enterprise-Wide Procurement

SF – Standard Form

SIC – Standard Industrial Classification

SOO – Statement of Objectives

SOW – Statement of Work

SSA – Source Selection Authority

T

TAA – Trade Agreements Act

T&M – Time and Materials

TINA – Truth in Negotiations Act

TO – Task Order

TOS – Terms of Service

U

UEI – Unique Entity Identifier

UFP – Uniform Federal Procurement

U.S.C. – United States Code

V

VA – Department of Veterans Affairs

VOSB – Veteran-Owned Small Business

W

WBS – Work Breakdown Structure

WOSB – Women-Owned Small Business

X, Y, Z

XYZ – Common placeholder for examples in government documentation

APPENDIX C: FEDERAL RFP SECTIONS

A **Federal Request for Proposal (RFP)** follows a standardized structure as outlined in **Federal Acquisition Regulation (FAR) Part 15.204-1**, which prescribes the uniform contract format (UCF). This structure is designed to ensure clarity, transparency, and consistency across all government solicitations. A federal RFP is divided into **13 sections**, each serving a distinct purpose in the proposal development process.

Sections of a Federal RFP:

Section A – Solicitation/Contract Form

This section provides the **basic information** about the solicitation, including the **RFP number, issuing agency, contracting officer, and proposal due date**. It may also include special notices, the type of contract being awarded (firm-fixed-price, cost-plus-fixed-fee, etc.), and signature blocks for government and contractor representatives.

Section B – Supplies or Services and Prices/Costs

This section outlines **the scope of work and pricing structure**. It includes Contract Line Item Numbers (**CLINs**), which define the **deliverables, quantities, unit pricing, and funding sources**. Contractors must fill out pricing details in accordance with these requirements.

Section C – Description/Specifications/Statement of Work (SOW)

This is the **technical heart of the RFP**. It details the **statement of work (SOW), performance work statement (PWS), or statement of objectives (SOO)**, which define **what is to be delivered, performance expectations, and any specific technical requirements**.

Section D – Packaging and Marking

This section specifies **how deliverables should be packaged, labeled, and shipped** to meet government standards, including requirements for hazardous materials, barcoding, and other logistical considerations.

Section E – Inspection and Acceptance

This section establishes **the government's quality assurance measures**, including **inspection, testing, and acceptance criteria**. It defines how the government will evaluate delivered products or services to ensure they meet contract requirements.

Section F – Deliveries or Performance

This section outlines **the timeline and conditions for delivery and performance**, specifying **milestones, schedules, and locations for work completion**. It may also include penalties for late deliveries and criteria for performance evaluations.

Section G – Contract Administration Data

This section includes administrative details such as **billing procedures, contract modifications, and invoice submission requirements**. It also identifies the **Contracting Officer (CO)** and **Contracting Officer's Representative (COR)** responsible for contract oversight.

Section H – Special Contract Requirements

This section covers **any additional special terms and conditions** that are not included in other sections. This may include **security clearances, key personnel requirements, subcontracting limits, intellectual property rights, and compliance with unique agency regulations**.

Section I – Contract Clauses

This section incorporates **mandatory FAR and agency-specific clauses** that govern contract execution. These clauses may include **termination rights, limitation of liability, confidentiality agreements, and wage determinations** (such as Service Contract Act compliance).

Section J – List of Attachments

This section provides a list of **all attachments, exhibits, and appendices** referenced in the RFP, including **technical drawings, specifications, past performance forms, and pricing templates**.

Section K – Representations, Certifications, and Other Statements of Offerors

This section requires offerors to submit **certifications and representations** verifying compliance with specific government regulations. These include **small business status, Buy American Act compliance, and conflict of interest disclosures**.

Section L – Instructions, Conditions, and Notices to Offerors

This section provides **detailed proposal submission instructions**, including formatting, page limitations, evaluation factors, and deadlines. It outlines **how proposals should be structured** and the submission process (electronic, hard copy, etc.).

Section M – Evaluation Factors for Award

This section details **how the government will evaluate proposals** and determine contract awards. It describes **evaluation criteria such as technical capability, past performance, price, management approach, and risk assessment**. It also specifies whether the award will be based on **Lowest Price Technically Acceptable (LPTA) or Best Value Trade-Off (BVTO) methodologies**.

Summary

A **Federal RFP consists of 13 sections**, each serving a **specific role in defining contract requirements, submission guidelines, and evaluation processes**. Understanding these sections is **critical for businesses competing in government contracting**. Mastering the structure of an RFP ensures that **proposals are compliant, competitive, and strategically aligned with government requirements**.

APPENDIX D: LIST OF RESOURCES AND SOURCES

This appendix provides a comprehensive list of resources and references used throughout this book, including government websites, regulatory databases, procurement tools, industry publications, and educational materials. These sources are invaluable for businesses seeking to navigate government contracting, stay updated on regulations, and enhance their bidding strategies.

Government Regulations and Procurement Resources

1. Federal Acquisition Regulation (FAR) – The primary regulation governing federal procurements.
   - Website: https://www.acquisition.gov/far
2. Defense Federal Acquisition Regulation Supplement (DFARS) – Regulations specific to Department of Defense (DoD) contracts.
   - Website: https://www.acq.osd.mil/dpap/dars/dfarspgi/current/index.html
3. Code of Federal Regulations (CFR) – Title 48 – The official codification of federal procurement rules.

- Website: https://www.ecfr.gov/current/title-48
4. System for Award Management (SAM.gov) – The official website for federal contract opportunities, entity registration, and awards.
    - Website: https://sam.gov
5. Small Business Administration (SBA) – Government Contracting Assistance – SBA's programs for small businesses, including 8(a), HUBZone, and WOSB certification.
    - Website: https://www.sba.gov/federal-contracting9o;
6. General Services Administration (GSA) eLibrary – The official source for GSA contract schedules.
    - Website: https://www.gsaelibrary.gsa.gov

Contracting and Bid Opportunity Databases

7. SAM.gov – Official database for all federal contract opportunities.
    - Website: https://sam.gov
8. GovWin IQ by Deltek – Market intelligence platform for tracking and winning government contracts.
    - Website: https://www.deltek.com/en/products/business-development/govwin
9. Beta.SAM.gov – FPDS (Federal Procurement Data System) – Data repository of historical government contracts.
    - Website: https://www.fpds.gov
10. USASpending.gov – Database of federal government spending, including awarded contracts.
    - Website: https://www.usaspending.gov
11. GSA Advantage! – Federal marketplace for contractors with GSA Schedule contracts.
    - Website: https://www.gsaadvantage.gov

Proposal Development and Capture Management Resources

12. Shipley Associates – Proposal Development and Capture Management
    - Website: https://www.shipleywins.com
13. APMP (Association of Proposal Management Professionals) – Professional association for proposal and business development professionals.
    - Website: https://www.apmp.org
14. NCMA (National Contract Management Association) – Organization providing training, certifications, and resources on government contracting.
    - Website: https://www.ncmahq.org
15. Govology – Training platform for small businesses entering the federal marketplace.
    - Website: https://govology.com

Certifications and Compliance Resources

16. Small Business Certifications (SBA 8(a), WOSB, HUBZone, SDVOSB) – Information on small business certifications and their benefits.
    - Website: https://www.sba.gov/federal-contracting/contracting-assistance-programs
17. CMMC (Cybersecurity Maturity Model Certification) – DoD cybersecurity compliance framework.
    - Website: https://www.acq.osd.mil/cmmc/
18. DCAA (Defense Contract Audit Agency) – Guidance on accounting and compliance for government contracts.
    - Website: https://www.dcaa.mil
19. NIST SP 800-171 – Cybersecurity compliance standards for contractors handling controlled unclassified information (CUI).

   ○ Website: https://csrc.nist.gov/publications/detail/sp/ 800-171/rev-2/final

Industry Events, Trade Shows, and Networking Opportunities

20. National Defense Industrial Association (NDIA) Conferences – Defense industry events and networking opportunities.
    ○ Website: https://www.ndia.org
21. AFCEA (Armed Forces Communications & Electronics Association) – Industry networking and training events for defense and intelligence contractors.
    ○ Website: https://www.afcea.org
22. Small Business Innovation Research (SBIR) and Small Business Technology Transfer (STTR) Programs – Federal funding opportunities for small businesses engaged in R&D.
    ○ Website: https://www.sbir.gov
23. AUSA (Association of the U.S. Army) Annual Meeting – A major event for businesses in defense contracting.
    ○ Website: https://www.ausa.org/annual
24. DLA (Defense Logistics Agency) Industry Days – Procurement events focused on supply chain opportunities with the DoD.
    ○ Website: https://www.dla.mil

Professional Development and Learning Resources

25. Defense Acquisition University (DAU) – Free training for government contractors and acquisition professionals.
    ○ Website: https://www.dau.edu
26. GSA Training for Vendors – Online and in-person training on selling to the government.
    ○ Website: https://www.gsa.gov/training-events

27. Coursera – Government Contracting and Procurement Courses – Online courses covering procurement fundamentals.
    - Website: https://www.coursera.org
28. Udemy – Proposal Writing and Capture Management Courses – Affordable training for writing federal proposals.
    - Website: https://www.udemy.com
29. LinkedIn Learning – Government Contracting Courses – Online training modules taught by industry professionals.
    - Website: https://www.linkedin.com/learning

Legal and Compliance Assistance

30. Procurement Technical Assistance Centers (PTACs) – Free counseling and training for small businesses.
    - Website: https://www.aptac-us.org
31. SCORE – Free Small Business Mentoring – Provides business mentorship and consulting.
    - Website: https://www.score.org
32. National Institute of Government Purchasing (NIGP) – Resources on public sector procurement practices.
    - Website: https://www.nigp.org
33. Department of Labor – Wage Determinations – Compliance guidelines for federal labor laws.
    - Website: https://www.dol.gov/agencies/whd/government-contracts

APPENDIX E: BIBLIOGRAPHY

Amrhein, Tom. *Failure to Lead, Leads to Failure - The Art of Proposal Management*. Journal of the Association of Proposal Management Professionals, Spring/Summer 2002.

Badgerow, Dana B., Gregory A. Garrett, Dominic F. DiClementi, and Barbara M. Weaver. *Managing Contracts for Peak Performance*. National Contract Management Association, Vienna, VA, 1990.

Bazerman, Max, and Margaret A. Neale. *Negotiating Rationally*. The Free Press, New York, 1992.